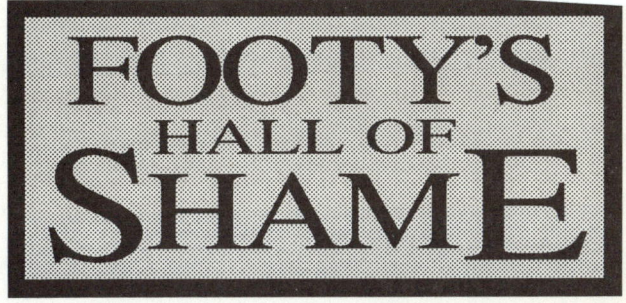

FOOTY'S HALL OF SHAME

BY

DAVE WARNER

WITH CARTOONS BY
STEVE PANOZZO

FREMANTLE ARTS CENTRE PRESS

First published 1996 by
FREMANTLE ARTS CENTRE PRESS
193 South Terrace (PO Box 320), South Fremantle
Western Australia, 6162.

Consulting editor B R Coffey.
Designed by John Douglass.
Production Coordinator Linda Martin.

Typeset by Fremantle Arts Centre Press
and printed by McPherson's Printing Group, Victoria.

National Library of Australia
Cataloguing-in-publication data

Warner, Dave, 1953 - .
Footy's hall of shame.

ISBN 1 86368 158 2.

1. Australian football — Humour. I. Title.

796.3360207

Department for
theArts
Western Australia

The State of Western Australia has made an investment in this project
through the Department for the Arts.

For
Dave McCurdy
who inducted me into the
mystery of the pigskin

ACKNOWLEDGEMENTS

Numerous players, past and present, media colleagues football officials, historians and fans helped provide the colour and statistics for the book.

I am indebted to the enormous assistance of Michelangelo Rucci of the *Adelaide Advertiser* for South Australian background and Les Everett for Western Australian material. Geoff Christian's West Australian contribution was also greatly appreciated. Central Districts, Norwood, West Adelaide, Sydney Swans and Subiaco Football Clubs must all be thanked for particular assistance, and Bob Uttenbroek and the East Fremantle Football Club were extremely generous with their contribution. Dave Clement is thanked for his statistical efforts. The WAFL, and Sam Siciliano in particular, were also of tremendous help.

A special thanks to Steve Panozzo, NOZ Productions, for the cartoons which appear throughout the text.

Every effort has been made to contact copyright holders and to obtain permission to use visual material included in this book. The publisher would appreciate advice of copyright ownership in cases where efforts have not been successful so that full acknowledgement may be included in any subsequent edition.

CONTENTS

THE DISHONOUR BOARD

FINALS FLOPS AND FADE-OUTS

CHEWY ON YA BOOT

DOG DAY AFTERNOONS

SUSTAINED MALEVOLENCE

BLOOPERS BY UMPIRES, LEAGUE OFFICIALS AND MEDIA

DOOM RECRUITS

AFTER HOURS

GUEST NOMINATIONS

CLUB DUD — CLUB BY CLUB LOWLIGHTS

Mum's the word.
(Tony Feder/ Sporting Pix.)

FOREWORD

by H G Nelson

In this day and age there are far too many unreadable sprays on the sports book market that celebrate AFL greats, the ten-goals-a-game players and the record-breaking feats. There are thin, weedy pamphlets that document the lives of the Brownlow, Magarey and Sandover Medal winners and all the wonderful occasions and friendships that life at the top of the AFL code has to offer. These puffs are hurled willy-nilly at the jaded football public. Coughed up by old players, retired coaches, boundary umpires, strappers, boot studders and commentators, not to mention issues from the tissue types who are always on the bleat about some searing issue that is threatening to ruin the game as we know it. They are drop-punted from the presses every time a goal umpire dashes for both flags.

What do we learn from these hastily cobbled together sprays? Bugger all. We know who was the greatest! Who was the best mark! Who was the funniest! Who had the biggest trouser trumpet! It is all in the footy *Record*. Or is discussed in depth every Monday on 'Talking Footy' with Bruce, Mike, Blighty and totally overwhelmed guests with very little to say.

With this magnificent monograph, *Footy's Hall of Shame*, David Warner has had the guts, the vision, the game plan and the arousal to end this tragic farce. You have a firm, yet caressing, grip on the only book in Australian football literature that celebrates The Dull, The Dud and The Dead. And doesn't it feel good.

This is a sprinkle that celebrates those who just turned up and played. It goes out of its way to champion those no one has bothered to remember. It revels in those who played seventy-three matches up-front and only bothered the scorer once, when a lucky point was snared as the ball rolled the wrong way. *Footy's Hall of Shame* pours a very large drink for the cod ordinary.

And what of its author, first picked in any side, Warner, D. is the perfect caretaker for *Footy's Hall of Shame*, as Dave's record is one that opens a lot of doors. As a player he could snag the tricky ones on the turn from fifty metres out. He could shark the 6 pointers from the pocket on his wrong side going away from the big sticks with a glorious banana off either foot. If the big men were tiring in the last quarter the coach could throw Dave on the ball and get a burst of winning go-forward grunt out of the centre. If you were up against traditional rivals and wanted to get a bushfire started early to pull the head off their big names, Dave could start a stink off-ball and have their Best and Fairest booked for an appearance Monday night before the tribunal. If there was a young bloke down from the bush Dave could always get him going with the oldie, but goodie, about how the coach was on the sideways samba with the lad's girlfriend and mother. Finally, Dave was very handy with what Javed Miandad used to call 'The Dirty Words'. And the lovely thing about Dave's game was that whatever Dave started he could finish. He was the complete footballer.

Once his playing days were over, Dave, naturally, became a coach. When he minced out for his first night on the job with the clipboard, The Acme Thunderer and the witches' hats, he reminded me so much of 'The Galloping Gasometer' Mick Nolan. Dave might have let down sharply from his 109-kilo playing weight once he slung the boots on the rusty nail in the dressing shed, but the complete football mind upstairs was ticking over ready to go off like a suitcase full of semtex. Dave was an ideas coach. It was all ideas, good ideas, new ideas, big ideas, match-winning ideas and Flag-winning ideas.

The team would turn up to training never knowing what to expect. After a big loss it might be nude night and a beach run buffed, with the club faithful lined up on the esplanade on the leer and jeer. Dave revolutionised the game with his three-quarter time addresses. I hope these slime-covered scuds from the throat will be published as a companion volume to this excellent read. Unfortunately his sight, sound and smell three-quarter time happenings featuring live quokkas, still flapping flathead fish and horribly acrid aromas that seemed to come from nowhere are not best captured on the printed page.

He would appear at the tribunal for all his players. He brought a little bit of old-fashioned show biz magic to proceedings which made the WAFL judiciary on a Monday night the hottest ticket in town. His revolutionary restaging of weekend incidents using professional actors were breathtaking. The record shows that Dave and his players appeared before the tribunal 349 times and his record was 17 weeks suspension in total. A *Guinness Book of Records* feat that has yet to be equalled.

Dave was always thinking about the game and it just was not a lot of front-bar spout. He followed through. For instance, to get over unsightly wrestling between the talls at boundary throw-ins, Dave came up with the novel wheeze of lying the opposing rucks on the ground one metre apart and have the boundary umpire roll the ball between them, and then allowing the Sherrin to be cleared only using the buttocks. A brilliant solution to this the game's greatest blight. So very, very watchable; big fit Australian men on the bot going at it hammer and tongs.

I know Dave would not want to claim complete credit for this yet-to-be-adopted innovation as it does borrow heavily on ideas Kevin Sheedy has been pushing in his column in the *Age*.

As you can see you are in safe hands with a man who knows his football, who can run hard at the ball all day, who can do the one per cent things, who can win the fight and win the match, and now all this experience is wrapped up in this book.

No, you have done yourself proud tracking this one down.

You can relax in the post-hooter bath with a large one handy. Go on you deserve it.

And remember just by bagging it, football is the winner.

Roo-meat.
(Tony Feder/Sporting Pix.)

INTRODUCTION

From the first time we're swaddled in garish colours and hauled off to be indoctrinated into the mystery of the pigskin, we have impressed upon us the game's outstanding achievements. So much is written about this honour board of Aussie Rules that each year it probably means one less Malaysian rainforest. Even as the tomato sauce coagulates on the season's first hot dog you can hear whispers in the crowd as proud fans recite their catechism.

Who holds the record for the most AFL games?

Michael Tuck, Hawthorn, with 426 holds the record for most games.

Which South Melbourne rover won three Brownlow Medals?

South Melbourne's Bob Skilton won three Brownlow Medals.

And so on.

Yet for all this documentation and ingestion there is a gaping hole in our footy diet. Namely, who makes it onto the DIShonour board? Who were the duds, the rats, the cheats and the inept who have played, officiated in or written about the game?

Surely they deserve a place in the annals of pigskin history?

How could we appreciate the three musketeers without Von Richlieu? Holmes without Moriarty? Abbot without Costello?

And so we bring you a tome to redress the balance, to ensure a deserved place in history is reserved for the villains, the skill-challenged and the integrity-impaired. We bring you FOOTY'S HALL OF SHAME.

However, we cannot emphasise enough that the Hall Of Shame has been compiled in the spirit of celebration not denigration.

Every footballer who has ever played a league game is a champion. Some players may be more champion that others but anyone who has made it onto a league field can be proud of their achievement.

Every player, umpire, committee person and fan enriches the game in their own way.

After all, it is the things and people that cause us to gnash our teeth in rage or double us over laughing that make the game human, that set it apart from choreographed gymnastics or dull accounting.

In the following pages we pay homage to the fears, follies and foibles that make Aussie Rules the greatest game of all.

Dave Warner

THE PLAYER HALL
OF SHAME

BUNGLE BUNGLE
THE WORST PLAYER MISTAKES

It isn't only the journeyman footballer that can made a game-losing error or the most fundamental of mistakes. Some great champions can find themselves inducted into the Hall Of Shame for one momentary lapse that makes us realise they are human after all.

JIM STYNES

It was Melbourne against Hawthorn in the 1987 Preliminary Final, and Melbourne had it in the bag; a Grand Final appearance, their first in 30-odd years; seconds to go.

This was the culmination of a fantastic late surge that had seen them make the finals. Idol Robbie Flower would finally make a Grand Final side in his last season and who knew, maybe fate would smile on the Demons and send them a flag?

Already having calculated which mates had MCG members' tickets, Demons fans could envisage their newly washed 4-wheel drives in the car park on the Big Saturday. They could almost taste the Moet and spatchcock.

And then big Jim Stynes ran across the mark as Gary Buckenara lined up from a mile out. The penalty took Buckenara within kicking range, the siren sounded and the Hawk made no mistake.

The dream vanished.

Irish jokes reigned for a week, Flower bowed out never having run onto the MCG for that one day in September, Jim Stynes had inducted himself into the Hall Of Shame.

Flower later summed up his feelings, 'The feeling of emptiness was indescribable. We had the game, now we'd lost.'

Stynes credited that nadir with giving him the determination to become a top player. In 1991 Stynes won the Brownlow

Medal and at the time of writing he is on track to surpass Skinny Titus' record run of 204 consecutive league games.

DICK LEE

Walter 'Dick' Lee was the first of the great Collingwood and Victorian full-forwards.

On 10 August, 1921, Dick Lee cost Victoria an Australian Championiship.

In a game against WA, Lee had a chance to put the Vics in front in the last minute of the game. He opted for his placekick specialty.

So deadly was Lee that amusement parks banned him from competing in their straight-kicking competitions for fear he would send them broke.

Writing in the *Sporting Globe* in the 1940s one of Lee's opponents, Richmond's Vic Thorp said of Lee: 'He was more than just a good footballer. He was above everything else a really quick thinker ... his anticipation and sense of the game were uncanny.'

All the more amazing then that in 1921 Lee blew it. When the ball which he had set for the placekick rolled, Lee picked it up and attempted to dash past his opponent.

Unfortunately for Lee that opponent was one of the greatest-ever Western Australian players, 'Nipper' Truscott. Truscott stripped Lee of the ball and dashed away.

WA won the game and the series.

POINT BLANK

Two of the finest players of the modern era, Brownlow Medallists GRAHAM MOSS and MALCOLM BLIGHT, both managed to induct themselves into the Hall Of Shame when they marked, turned and at point-blank range ... kicked a behind.

Moss was playing for Claremont at the time of his bungle and Blight for North Melbourne. Each mistook the line between goal and point post for the goal line.

THE BLIND LEADING THE BLIND

Subiaco's PETER MUNROE was a great model for the kids: he always kept his eye on the ball.

This was because Munroe was more short-sighted than a State government roads plan. Nobody knew of his disability for a long time, however, it turned out he had lost his contact lens and didn't want to tell the club.

Munroe confided his most embarrassing moment to his team-mates. Playing for Footscray against South Melbourne he had suddenly hared across the ground followed by a puzzled Francis Jackson — the only player in the league with worse eyesight than Munroe!

Right in front of the members stand Munroe had then leapt into the air and tried to mark a seagull. When the crowd burst out laughing the embarrassed player had pretended it was a joke until confessing later that his eyesight was so bad he had thought it was the ball.

Munroe managed to liven up a club wherever he went. He brought with him to Subiaco a mate from Darwin, named Flash. Munroe told Subiaco coach Ken Armstrong that Flash was a magic bloke who could play anywhere. Moreover he had a special gift that he would like to display to the players. The assembled players were curious as Flash took the stage and dropped his daks to reveal his was endowed with three testicles.

The mystery of the third testicle was most likely explained by the fact that Norwood's MICHAEL POULTER, also from Darwin, only had one!

Poulter had a particular fondness for port.

Not the sort you play but the sort you drink. Not beyond having a pre-game nip, one day he sortied a little too far into a fine blend. In flying for a speccy he managed to miss the mark and hit the ball with his head, thereby adding the header dimension so long lacking in our great game.

THE WRONG MAN

At half-time in the 1979 WAFL Derby Grand Final, East Fremantle were doing it easily over South. The driving force for the Blue and Whites was BRIAN PEAKE who, as always, was wearing number 7.

One can imagine that South's coach Mal Brown gave a half-time address that emphasised physical commitment.

The third quarter was in its first stanza when a pack cleared to reveal an inert East Fremantle player on the ground: Wayne Cormack, who wore number 17.

Maybe it was the success of The Grateful Dead back then that inspired Cormack, like Peake, to wear a beard. Whatever it was, with the beard and a 7 on his back, he was reasonably similar to his team-mate in appearance, although he had not had the influence on the game that his team-mate had.

Cormack was carted off and sent straight to hospital with a jaw in more pieces than the ALP caucus debating uranium.

The culprit was identified as South's muscle-bound reserve Dale Reeves who had only just come onto the ground. In an echo of Duncan Wright (*see WRIGHT-SOMMERVILLE*) this was the last game Reeves was to play with South.

If the conclusion drawn by most, that Reeves meant to get Peake and got Cormack, is correct then Reeves makes it doubly into our Hall Of Shame.

Not only for the king-hit, but for getting the wrong man.

BORN LOSERS

Somewhere in their past life these players and institutions must have slain an albatross. Into the Hall Of Shame 'losers' category, though no reflection on their playing ability, we are forced to induct the following:

JONAHS

RENE KINK (Collingwood, Essendon and St Kilda, 1973-86) nicknamed 'The Hulk' because of his resemblance to Marvel Comics' gamma-rayed mutant, played in 6 losing Grand Finals.

With thighs thicker than Homer Simpson and pecs more developed than the Gold Coast, Kink always looked more suited to 'Gladiators' than footy. That he played as long as he did, at the level he did, surprised the mugs in the outer. Tom Hafey allegedly blamed Kink for costing the Pies the tied 1977 Grand Final.

Whether or not that is true or fair, the fact remains that Renee 'walked away' 6 times without a premiership medal.

PAUL WESTON played in 6 losing Grand Finals before a win.

To be fair, the first 5 came with Glenelg, a team that loses Grand Finals like league coaches lose hair.

But Weston couldn't blame the club when in 1983 he moved to Essendon and copped an 83-point Hawthorn Grand Final thrashing.

Weston was saved from replacing Renee Kink as the most-losingest Grand Finalist when in 1984 the Baby Bombers got up and beat Hawthorn.

OWN GOAL

St Kilda's BRIAN WALSH is the only player in AFL/VFL history to score a goal for the opposition.

The goal umpire made a mistake in a 1958 match and ensured permanent ignominy for Walsh.

The Saints' opponents that day? Carlton of course.

(As we go to press in May 1996, the West Coast Eagles are claiming another such mistake involving Eagles rover TONY EVANS. Again the opponents were Carlton.

LORD I WAS NOT BORN A GAMBLING MAN

If ex-South Fremantle captain GARY SCOTT ever steps into a two-up ring, bet against him. He'd be the only bloke who could drop a cat and have it land on its back.

In 1963-4 Scott made more wrong calls than a myopic dyslexic in a vandalised phone box. Scott lost the toss on 21 consecutive occasions, finally winning against Swan Districts.

Poor ROBBIE FLOWER. One of the Demons' greats, Flower played 271 games before making his finals debut in 1987. Melbourne fell in the Preliminary Final against Hawthorn, denying him the chance of playing in a Grand Final (*see BUNGLE BUNGLE – JIM STYNES*).

BRIAN ROYAL

Brian Royal was marooned on 199 games when he did an Achilles tendon in round 20 of 1993, ending his career. Besides missing the 200-game milestone, the Footscray rover never got to play in a Grand Final, but he did play for the State and win the Dogs' Best and Fairest in 1983.

TUMBLING DICE
GAMBLING AND THE PIGSKIN

Wherever you have a sport you will have gambling. Aussie Rules is no exception.

Certain events have, from time to time, been tainted with the hint that results were 'fixed'. Sometimes the claims have been substantiated, sometimes not.

These days, even a minor gambling infraction creates headlines but at the turn of the century gambling was rife. With football a hugely popular game and players poorly remunerated by the clubs and often relying on individual patronage, the set-up was more like boxing than today's regimented and well-audited leagues.

Like boxing, there was a big profit for any gambler who could get a 'fix' in.

In Victoria allegations of playing 'dead' were relatively common until after the First World War, and several sensational cases sent reverberations wherever the code was played.

History has seen to it that the players mentioned below, rightly or wrongly have been inducted into the Hall Of Shame as integrity-challenged.

THE CHEATS

JACK McINERNEY

In 1895 Collingwood was rocked to its foundations when player George Williams complained officially that one of Collingwood's key players, rover Jack McInerney, had tried to persuade him both before and during a match, to play dead. He alleged McInerney had been bribed to ensure a Collingwood defeat.

The news leaked from the committee room the next day and Williams was set upon by toughs in Johnson Street and badly beaten.

The Official Centenary of the Collingwood Football Club notes that there was no doubt the incidents were related, so one can only imagine that the thugs had a few quid against the Pies and were not impressed by Williams' integrity.

Williams' evidence was accepted by the committee and McInerney was dismissed from the club.

Over the next four years Collingwood blocked every attempt by McInerney to return to football. Finally, in 1899 when Prahran joined the VFA, he was allowed back.

ALEX 'BONGO' LANG

Carlton's Alex 'Bongo' Lang (1906-10 and 1916-17) is described in *The Encylopedia of League Footballers* as a clever rover whose dash and persistence made him one of the best in the league.

In 1909 the *Australasian* ranked him as the outstanding player in the competition — which only goes to show how great was the fall experienced by this 'Joe Jackson' of Aussie Rules.

When Lang and two team-mates were pulled from the team just before the 1910 Second Semi-Final against South Melbourne, a number of Carlton players threatened to walk out, but Carlton committeemen moved from player to player urging them to do their best.

The word was Lang and his cronies had been offered £100 to throw the game.

When subsequently charged with accepting a bribe to 'play dead', Lang claimed that he had immediately backed Carlton but such sleight of hand was not considered a satisfactory defence and Lang was found guilty and given a 5-year suspension from the game. In the same purge, Doug Fraser, an 11-game Carlton ingenue, also copped a 5-year plan from the VFL.

The third player was cleared of any wrongdoing and re-instated.

That Lang actually came back to play after he had served his penalty says much for his resilience. It is a great SHAME that Bongo Lang will be primarily remembered as the game's greatest cheat.

TOMMY BAXTER

Tommy Baxter was one of the heroes of Collingwood's 1910 premiership (*see DOG DAY AFTERNOONS*). Originally found guilty of fighting and suspended for a year after that Grand Final, he was amazingly exonerated at the re-hearing where it was claimed his report was a case of mistaken identity.

Collingwood's joy at having their star back for 1911 lasted about as long as the king prawns at a buffet.

The Grand Final of 1911 was as close as a boilermaker's singlet. Collingwood and Essendon were scrapping, both sides trying to get the upper hand.

With his team trailing by 3 points, Baxter twice missed easy shots for goal and once kicked into the man on the mark. Essendon got 2 goals to sneak away but Baxter kicked a sharp-angled goal with 4 minutes to go and closed the gap.

Moments later Baxter again had a chance to score but kicked into the man and then missed yet another easy shot. The bell rang with Essendon 1-goal winners.

Baxter was shunned by team-mates and hooted by fans as he walked from the field.

A known gambler and associate of the notorious John Wren, Baxter's background added to suspicion that he had 'played dead'.

Though exonerated by a subsequent committee hearing, the suspicion of foul play remained. In Baxter's defence it was pointed out that the conditions were atrocious and that he had been responsible for great mid-field play. Unfortunately, just like in that 1911 gluepot, Tommy Baxter discovered that mud sticks.

AND THE SNEAKS

Some players don't really deserve the title of 'cheat'. They don't actually break rules but just bend them enough so they and their integrity can 'sneak' through unscathed ... with a little extra cash.

ADJUSTING THE ODDS

JOHN GEROVICH was a sneak in more ways than one. Yes, he was a goal sneak capable of a miraculous mark. But he was sneaky in other ways too.

In 1959 WA travelled to play Tasmania after being walloped by the Vics by a mammoth 178 points the weekend before.

Tasmania had vastly different fortunes in the lead-up, triumphing over a Victoria B team. This situation led to odds of 5/4 being offered about the Sandgropers, and that was something that mercurial full-forward John Gerovich and footy writer Geoff Christian could not resist. They scraped together their last £20, a big sum in those days, and invested on a WA win. Gerovich was an obsessive punter, habitually carrying a racecard down his footy sock so he could check the race-results from the scoreboard during a game.

At half-time in the State game Christian was having kittens. WA were trailing Tassy and playing uninspired footy. The footy writer got beside Gerovich in the change rooms and spelled out the dire predicament — they didn't even have enough for a hot dog if they lost. The full-forward was unperturbed, telling Christian to go and borrow another £20 off team manager Frank Fuhrman.

'Another twenty?' spluttered Christian.

'Yea,' said Gerovich. 'We should be 2/1 by now.'

Gerovich cut lose in the second half and WA won by a big margin.

AND THE MEEK

SELF DEFEATING

West Coast Eagles TROY UGLE had a shot for goal after the final siren at Carlton. The Eagles had won the game and there was no need to take it, but Ugle went back and lined-up the near impossible shot. Ugle let loose with a magnificent kick which went through for a major. As his team-mates jumped for joy and slapped him on the back, Ugle's head was hung down and he was muttering to himself all the way to the change rooms.

When his mates asked him what the matter was he confessed he had made a wager and had the points spread exactly right before he'd taken the kick. His goal had blown him out of the water.

'Why didn't you just kick it out on the full?' they asked, bewildered.

'Ah Mick (Malthouse) would have known. He would have got me,' said Ugle.

Given the conditions that day and the difficulty of the kick, there was more chance of Elle McPherson being appointed to the Literature Board than of Malthouse finding out his player had deliberately missed.

COTTONWOOL

NEWTOWN Football Club's opponents could not believe it. Here it was three-quarter time and they were slaughtering Newtown. But over in the Newtown huddle a huge cheer had erupted and players were dancing with one another and jumping up and down on the spot. What on earth was happening?

What was happening was this. Newtown Football Club coach Gary 'Dinga' Towle had been told during the week there was a 'good thing' going at the track that weekend. He would be notified on the day and could make his betting arrangements accordingly.

'Dinga' convinced the players that with half of their trip fund as a stake, they could find themselves in Bali for 2 weeks instead of Woy Woy. Everybody had agreed they should put the trip fund on the 'good thing'. This was the reason for the three-quarter time elation. The 'good thing' had duly won and the players had been listening to the race on the tranny.

They finished the orange break, got clobbered in the last quarter but left the ground with a spring in their step.

Until they got to the boundary line. That was when dreams of Bali turned to images of Dubbo and dust.

The 'good thing' had been disqualified and the trip fund was now defunct.

The name of the 'good thing' was Fine Cotton, the horse that has been the centre of an ongoing scandal ever since.

FORGET ME SOONS
INAUSPICIOUS DEBUTS

Playing for Carlton in 1915, ex-Ballarat player JOE SHORTHILL was reported for kicking. Shorthill defended himself with all the eloquence of George 'The Animal' Steele, telling the tribunal he didn't know the difference between a kick and a trip.

In his debut, South Melbourne's LEN 'MOTHER' MORTIMER (1906-15, 289 goals in 153 games) dug a hole for a placekick and wished he had crawled into it when he kicked his placekick straight into the man on the mark.

Talk about running the gamut. In 1993 MATTHEW POWELL of the Crows had his first kick in AFL go out on the full. His next kick was a goal — and not long after that he was stretchered from the ground after a heavy collision.

TED WHITTEN was also stretchered from the ground in his debut, courtesy of Mopsy Fraser. The young Master Football had made the mistake of kicking a goal on the war dog (*see BELLIGERENT 7*).

WITH FRIENDS LIKE THESE
TERRIBLE TEAM-MATES

Sometimes team-mates can be your worst enemy. For inhumanity to their fellows the following are inducted into the Hall Of Shame:

There must be something in those colours of black and white. Collingwood's DICK CONDON (*see UMPIRES*) was notorious as both a player and coach for 'snotting' his own men. Condon caused dissention at Collingwood in equal measure to great success. He then took his formula to Richmond where he repeated the dose.

While with the Magpies PHIL CARMAN was often on report for causing mayhem, but on one occasion when he caused serious injury in full view of the umpires he got away with it. Maybe that's because the victim was team-mate Ron Wearmouth. Carman went to punch the ball and broke Wearmouth's nose instead ... at least, so he claimed.

Another black-and-white team, Swan Districts, were going through an awful patch in the late 1960s. They probably reached their nadir when one of their champions, JOHN TURNBULL, rolled around on the ground wrestling with a team-mate totally ignoring the ball.

GRAHAM ARTHUR (Hawthorn) is another who gave a team-mate a hard time. GARY YOUNG (Hawthorn, 1956-65) had his career ended when an Essendon player crashed into him resulting in a perforated bowel and peritonitis. As he lay on the ground Arthur ran past and said, 'Get up you weak bastard.'

RON TODD finished with 999 career goals in VFL and VFA. Who was the lousy bastard that didn't pass to him during that final game? Whoever you are, consider yourself SHAMED.

GIVEN THE BOOT

In the 1970s a group of NORWOOD players were in the habit of celebrating. One player who had not been accepted by the group because of his prudish behaviour, decided he should let it all out and join in.

A number of vodkas later, a paralytic puking mess, he was

removed from the premises of celebration by his team-mates. As they had not yet finished their revelry and as the sozzled Redleg was likely to throw up in any vehicle used as a holding pen, his team-mates dumped him in the boot of one of the cars.

The team-mates drank themselves into oblivion and it wasn't until they had woken from their own slumber hours later that somebody recalled the body in the boot.

When rescued the bewildered and terrified Redleg was in worse shape than Roseanne after a pig out. Covered in every form of human excrement, the poor soul was brought back into the world like a screaming infant.

Shame on you lads for the distress you caused your poor team-mate.

BROWN STAINS

MAL BROWN makes it into the Hall Of Shame for his consummate belligerence to players, umpires and officials, but he also makes it in this category. In 1967 Brown refused to train with team-mate ANGUS HORWOOD because he was too rough. Horwood once wrestled a shark he had hooked on his line before throwing it up on the beach at Geraldton.

It was that sort of aggression that had Brown storming off the training track voicing complaints to the team manager. When Horwood was traded to Subiaco the following season many believed it was to pacify the East Perth star.

PRE-MATCH NERVES

The worst case of pre-match nerves must be that of Subiaco's JEREMY McGRADE.

Just after the start of the 1979 season, Subiaco coach Peter Burton contacted promising amateur player Jeremy McGrade and invited him to training. McGrade explained he didn't think he was physically prepared for league, and as he was studying, he would stay with his amateur club.

Burton said he appreciated that but convinced McGrade to train for a week and have a run with the reserves. As the amateur season was still a week off McGrade consented, finding himself up against a young John Ironmonger in the 2s.

That week, Subiaco's league side got flogged.

The next week, McGrade went back and trained with his amateur club. When he got home after training and a couple of beers he learned that he had been chosen to play league against South Fremantle. McGrade was due to line-up on Basil Campbell — a player so tough and so mean he put a recording of footsteps in Ray Bauskis' walkman (only joking). Campbell was mean though and McGrade, obviously not without brains, refused to play.

He continued as an amateur and attracted attention from a number of VFL clubs, with both South Melbourne and Collingwood flying him over for the Grand Final. McGrade never did try and make the McGrade however and played amateurs until 1992.

Another youngster with definite thoughts was East Perth's BRUCE McKNIGHT. McKnight did not take kindly to being dragged from the ground in a game against East Fremantle at Perth Oval in 1992. McKnight packed his bags and left at half-time. That severed ties between the Royals and McKnight who now plays for South Fremantle.

WHAT'S UP DOC?

When DARREN 'THE DOC' WHEILDON was playing for Fitzroy in 1993 he was fined by the tribunal after being found guilty of shaking a goal post — even more extraordinary was the fact that it was his team-mate who was having a shot for goal at the time!

Maybe the Doc just wanted to make sure he won Fitzroy's goal kicking that year?

Or maybe he was still shaking with rage after the Roys

dropped him for the previous match when he failed to attend a handball competition at a TV studio?

THE HUNTER HUNTED

KEN HUNTER (Claremont, Carlton) and JIM KRAKOUER (Claremont, North Melbourne, St Kilda) got into an altercation while playing together at Claremont. Graham Moss, who was coaching at the time, sent Hunter into the change rooms to cool things down, but Jimmy, not one to let things go, continued the feud in the rooms.

Jim's brother, Phil, and some others stepped in to peace-make and hostilities ceased for about as long as it takes Roseanne to wolf down a hot-dog. As Hunter headed for his car in the car park, Jimmy was still keen to pursue a pugilistic outcome.

But Hunter made good his exit and it was thought that was the end of the matter.

In the early hours of the morning though, Claremont President Wally Maskiell received a phone call from a worried Hunter. Jimmy and some cronies had his place staked out.

Maskiell had to drive over to the seige and tap on Jimmy's window to talk reason and get the matter finally resolved.

ONE STUD SHORT OF THE FULL BOOT

We know footy players aren't meant to be rocket scientists but sometimes a bit of common sense might not go astray. In the category of 'one stud short of the full boot' we regretfully induct the following:

The Eagles match committee were stricken with panic when the call came: star Ashley McIntosh had terrible abdominal pains and was absolutely unable to move from his bed.

They rushed to the player's side and began a quick interrogation to determine what had caused this. If it was food poisoning, it might have repercussions for all the other players.

Carefully they went through the Eagle's diet with him — he was, after all, a known big eater.

Had he eaten something not on the list? A curry? Enchilada? Something naughty like that and likely to contain salmonella or some other dirty bug.

No. Ashley was adamant, he had not strayed from the complex carbohydrate diet. All he had was his pasta, water and some bread rolls.

'How many bread rolls?' somebody had the presence of mind to ask.

'Oh, sixteen or seventeen,' replied the wounded Eagle.

WARWICK CAPPER

When TV Sports man Cameron Williams was working up on the Gold Coast, he had an arrangement to meet Warwick Capper over some story or other.

Williams went to the high-rise apartment where Capper lived, found the door open and called out.

'Come on in,' yelled Warwick.

Williams could not, at first, locate the star full-forward. Eventually he spotted him on his balcony leaning way, way back, apparently unconcerned at the twenty-plus floor drop to the earth below.

'What the hell are you doing?' asked the bewildered journalist.

Capper held up a TV remote control. 'I'm seeing how far away you can have this thing and still change channels,' replied the goal sneak.

Yet another story concerns Capper and some missing airline baggage.

When the Swans arrived in Vancouver to play Melbourne, Capper's bags were the only ones missing. That the star attraction was in a strange city without any duds, bar what he was wearing, was of some concern to the promoters who wanted everything to go smoothly. They gave Capper several hundred dollars to fit himself out, fully expecting socks, jocks, shirt and trousers to be purchased. But Warwick had no need of such mundane clobber.

He returned from his shopping spree with one item: a spectacular jacket.

PERCY JONES

Carlton's Percy Jones, a player so erudite that he probably sledged Robert Dippierdemenico in Latin, ran for election with the slogan 'Point Perc At The Parliament'.

When coaching Carlton, Jones gathered his charges during a close game.

'I've only got two words to say,' urged Percy. 'Try real hard.'

WOW JONES

Legend has it that as a youngster in Castlemaine, Jones was adding to his tattoos when he looked across the road and spied some interesting Chinese scrawl on the window of the Chinese restaurant across the way. Jones had the tattooist copy the characters onto his body. When they were complete he took himself over to the restaurant and enquired of the proprietor what he had just adorned his body with.

'Oh, that's this week's special, sweet and sour dim-sims,' said the Chinaman.

Another Jones legend is that when the wife of the Carlton

President asked Wow how he got his nickname, he explained that he had a W tattooed on each cheek of his bum.

Wow's bum also features in another incident. Allegedly Carlton were on an end-of-season trip in the States and were on a training run through the hotel grounds when Wow got the call of nature. Wow discreetly took himself off behind a bush, did his business and rejoined the group — unaware that the opaque glass of the building against which he had toileted was one-way. On the other side were the 5-star patrons having their breakfast.

JIM VAN GOUGH

During the '80s, the end-of-season sojourn to London for the Foster's exhibition match was, without doubt, the plum in the orchard of administrators' perks.

Of prime importance was to make sure the AFL and Fosters' logos were painted prominently onto the grass of the venue; The Oval at Kennington in South London.

As Carlton's JIM BUCKLEY was a house painter, some bright spark came up with the idea of him doing the job. Buckley, after all, played for Carlton, and Fosters' supremo John Elliot was a Carlton man. Everybody would be happy.

Buckley painted the oval a treat. The logos sparkled like the duco of a new ferrari. As well they should, because Buckley had used enamel paint.

Several members of Surrey County Cricket Club, whose home is The Oval, are believed to have suffered apoplexy on arriving at the ground for the opening fixture of the County season and seeing the logos still smiling brightly.

Some 6 months later during the cricket season, the logos, barely faded, still adorned the mid-wicket boundary.

WIDE RECEIVERS

Some players don't seen to thrive on the hurly-burly of the game. They prefer the wide open spaces where their skills can operate with the minimum of harassment. Unfortunately some fans mistake this cunning strategy as an unwillingness to put life and limb on the line for the club. It is time that 'time-out' was called on such notions and those in the club of the 'wide-receivers' hauled out from the pit of shame into which they have been unjustifiably cast by blood-thirsty fans looking for 'fist' instead of 'fast'. Once more into the bright light of stardom into which they truly belong we drag the following:

TRUTH WILL OUT

West Perth's STEPHEN SMEATH played numerous fine games during the '60s and '70s for West Perth, and though many opposition players suspected that Smeathy might be a bit 'frightened' they just could never get close enough to the long-striding quiff to find out.

Really they had no chance of closing down a practised greyhound like Smeath, whose evasive skills had been honed from schooldays when tormentors (later to be West Perth team-mates) had chased him from the Mount Hawthorn oval and down the street to his house.

In an amazing twist of events Smeath was once reported for kicking Williams of East Fremantle, who in turn was reported for striking Smeath. Where had the reporting umpire been during Stephen's career? Mars? Or the pub?

The tribunal heard Smeath's evidence — yes he had felt a blow, no he hadn't kicked Williams, just raised his knee in self-defence. The tribunal knew the truth when they heard it. Smeath cleared, Williams suspended.

ALLEN 'SHORTY' DANIELS (Claremont and Footscray) was another suspected by even his own fans of being 'terrified'. In fact the Footscray faithful had nicknamed him 'Terra' for that reason.

Shorty, however, had no doubts of his aggression at the ball and in fact can point to two reports in 1983 and 1984 as proof of his 'take no prisoners' attitude. In 1983 he was suspended for 1 week for hitting East Fremantle's Kevin Taylor, in 1984 he was cleared of another strike charge.

At half time during Daniels' tenure at the Western Oval the Footscray crowd erupted into spasms of laughter. The reason? In the little league there was a blond-headed young girl wearing the number 5 Footscray jumper, the same number as Shorty.

UN-SHAMED

Sometimes players have been inducted into football's shameland incorrectly. We hereby send in the chopper to winch them from the pit into which they have been unjustifiably hurled.

JOE SMITH

In a close game at Claremont, with his team trailing, Claremont's Joe Smith took a mark just 15 metres out when the final siren went.

Smith had the chance of winning the game; the white wine in the Claremont members area was in mid-sip — could they win it?

To the amazement of everybody at the oval, Smith, instead of taking his shot, went for a short pass. The wine glasses slipped from the stricken hands and shattered on the harsh reality: Claremont had lost a game they might have won.

Joe Smith was reduced to pants-down-hall-of-shame-dunce status. His name entered footy vernacular as synonymous with stupidity: a kick into the man on the mark, a bad handpass, any wrong option became a 'Joe Smith'.

It transpires that it was team-mate David Muir who yelled at Smith to play on, and therefore it is Muir who ought to enter footy's folklore as a dill.

From now on, any shameful piece of footy strategy or execution will become known as a 'Muir'.

TREVOR SPRIGG

In the last round of 1968 Subiaco played East Fremantle, and Subiaco's Austin Robertson kicked 15 goals to break Bernie Naylor's long-standing season goal-kicking record of 156 goals.

East Fremantle's Trevor Sprigg is usually written-up as being the opponent who had all those goals kicked on him. Sprigg, in fact, was on Robertson for his last 2 goals but prior to that had been playing up the ground at centre half-forward.

We hereby un-shame Trevor Sprigg for this shocker on 'Ocker'.

CLUB MAD

OR HOW PLAYERS, COACHES AND OFFICIALS DIVED INTO THE HALL OF SHAME

SLACK ON THE TRACK

As long as training has been around players have found ways to avoid or minimise it. Legend and numerous are accounts of players going on orienteering jaunts and catching cabs home, sneaking out for drinks the night before a game, faking their fitness tests, feigning injury and so on. Nominated for the Hall Of Shame for particularly devious or blatant efforts are:

NORWOOD

After numerous successes back in the 1880s, the Norwood players began to resent the fundamentals such as training. Club officials were aghast when they realised that the skating rink they had rented for players' training at £20 was deserted. The President commented, 'It was with great reluctance that the committee was forced to admit that after the trip to Victoria it was an accomplished fact that the training energy of the players rapidly evaporated and the attendance at the training ground grew smaller week by week until, at last, it was deserted.'

TOO CONSCIENTIOUS

Being too much of a training 'consc' is every bit as shameful as being too slack. Richmond's JOHN ANNEAR used to love to prove himself the fittest and most-committed of the bunch, winning every training run during his Punt Road tenure. On one occasion Annear was held up on the way to training and the others decided to push off without him so the fitness fanatic would miss out on a 'win'. They were halfway round the circuit (the Yarra banks) when Annear arrived and saw them. Unable to catch them on foot Annear plunged into the murky waters, swam to the opposite bank, joined the pack and still led them home! If that's not worthy of a Hall Of Shame nomination what is?

DALE WEIGHTMAN

Dale 'The Flea' Weightman was not reknowned as a trainer or scholar so when Francis Burke conceived a 30-point game plan and sat his players down for a test, the whole room was flummoxed when the one hand to rise confidently to answer questions was that of the Flea.

Unerringly the Flea answered those questions nobody else was capable of.

Only when the suitably impressed coach had left the room did Dale reveal he had the 30-point plan taped to the back of the chair in front!

Dale was not so brilliant after his Tassie and Simpson Medal wins of 1985. The Tiger was out for a big night on the town and wisely decided at the after-match he should entrust the medals to team-mate Tim Gepp. Weightman had a night on the town that made Caligula look like Rev. Fred Nile.

Gepp made sure that the Simpson and Tassie Medals were safely stowed and brought them back to Melbourne. He wondered though why Dale did not approach him for them. Nearly a week had passed and still the Flea had not approached Gepp for his medals. Gepp was frightened to broach the subject, obviously something major had happened to make Flea hate those medals.

Finally after training, the Flea called Gepp over and whispered confidentially, 'Geppy, I'm stuffed.'

'What's the matter, Flea?' asked Gepp.

'I'm bloody almost too ashamed to tell you Geppy,' said the Flea. 'You wouldn't bloody read about it. I lost me medals that night back in Perth.'

When the SWANS first played in Sydney they were flying a number of players up every week. On occasions, a player would come up to play league whom none of the other players had ever met. Dennis Carroll, the only man to have been officially associated with the Swans prior to the move and all the time since, recalls that once on the main training run of the week there were only six Swans on the track! Flu had swept through the Sydney-based players and no Melbourne-based players were in attendance.

GET READY TO STRIP

When the SWANS arrived for their first game ever against the Eagles in Perth, they were expecting to get off the plane, have a light run, get the feel of the oval and go back to the hotel for an early night. So when the plane touched down and team management announced, 'Get ready to strip' they were all ready for some circuit work. It turned out the match committee had a different sort of activity in mind. The Swans went to the hotel where stripping sensation Baby Doll was appearing. Into the squash and with a solid counter meal to go — none of that pasta and other stuff, but old-fashioned steak and chips — the Swans players partook of the local custom.

Obviously the match committee's strategy acclimatised them to local conditions for they won the match against the Eagles after what must have been one of the strangest pre-match build-ups of all time.

THE LAMEST EXCUSES

For the worst excuses for missing training we nominate the following and induct the players into the Hall Of Shame:

DETECTIVE DYER

RAY POULTER (Richmond 1946-56) worked for a league umpire and always arrived late for training. He told his coach, Jack Dyer, that the umpire disliked Dyer and wouldn't let Poulter go early. Smelling a rat the size of one of Mopsy Fraser's fists, Dyer, in Sam Spade tradition, followed Poulter after he had knocked off work and watched while he went home for over an hour. Maybe Dyer threatened Poulter with his John Roscoe, for thereafter Poulter was punctual.

A LOT OF BANK

AUSTIN ROBERTSON JNR, the Subiaco and South Melbourne full-forward, coached East Sydney Rules Club for a time when he moved to the harbour city. Austin, a wine-and-cheese man, never used to come back to the beery, pokie-machine atmosphere of the Easts' Rules Club during the week ... or so the players thought. One Monday after training was the exception that proved the rule. Austin wandered in to find Danny, one of his absentee players, propping up the bar.

'Danny, you weren't on the track today?' enquired Robertson.

'Not today coach, no. It's a bank holiday,' replied Danny.

'But you don't work in a bank.'

'No,' said Danny, 'but I've got my money in one.'

FOLLOW THE LEADER

During a South Melbourne time trial, NEVILLE FIELDS and JOHN ROBERTS were sprung taking a short cut.

When Fields was called on to explain, he owned up. He admitted he had no chance of making his time so he had taken the short cut.

The coach took that on board and asked Roberts, 'What about you?'

'Well, I was only following the bloke in front of me,' exclaimed Roberts.

THUNDER AND BLUNDER
THE MOST EMBARRASSING EFFORTS OF COACHES AND OFFICIALS

Coaches and officials are not beyond inducting themselves into the Hall Of Shame. Even some of the greats find themselves there. Here are a few self-inflicted splinters from the bench.

JOHN TODD has been one of the WAFL's most successful-ever coaches (East Fremantle, Swan Districts, South Fremantle, West Coast Eagles — 5 WAFL premierships). He also coached a composite Australian team, The Galahs, against Ireland.

One of the most disciplinarian of all coaches in the code, Todd has on occasion gone just too far.

While coaching Swan Districts he clocked player Kevin Caton during the team huddle. Caton became Todd's son-in-law so one can only wonder what was said the next day over the Sunday roast.

Toddy was also one of the combatants in a panel-show stoush. Perth radio 6PR used to hold these panel shows of a Friday afternoon in the convivial atmosphere of Perth's suburban pubs. Todd and fellow-panellist Rod Brown, President of the West Perth footy club, had a disagreement over some matter and suddenly the chairs were flying.

Nor did Toddy take too kindly to losses. After a string of embarrassing Eagles' losses he once trained his team so hard that Paul Peos collapsed and required medical treatment.

A Todd innovation was 'night training'. The Eagles would arrive in Melbourne, go for a run and 'pretend' to pass an imaginary ball to one another. When Troy Ugle jumped the fence and ran off into the night the coach yelled, 'Where do you think you're going?'

'I kicked the ball out on the full and I've just gone to fetch it,' cracked Ugle.

Perhaps the most amusing story concerning Todd though, is told by Dermott Brereton about a Galahs' tour of Ireland. Not long into the match Brereton was yanked by Todd and given a blast for being a bighead and not trying. Dermott waited patiently for his chance to go back on but half-time came and he was still on the sidelines. Going through the stats at half-time while hot-gospelling, Todd roasted two players in particular. He highlighted Dermott's paltry return and warned him not to expect he'd get a chance in the second half. Then he turned on Gary Buckenara. 'And you Bucky, you haven't had a single touch so far.'

'I might have half-a-chance if you put me on the ground,' replied Buckenara, who'd been warming the bench the entire half.

MATH MURDER

Taking training, NORM ROGERS (East Fremantle coach, 1968) told his charges, 'I want half you blokes to go over there, half to come here and the other half to come with me.'

Ex-Melbourne ruckman-forward 'BIG' BOB JOHNSON, who coached East Fremantle from 1962-66, was another not so good with maths. In one match he had 19 players on the field. By the time the opposition complained and the umpires lined the men up to count them, Bob had managed to send his extra man to the sidelines in a dressing-gown.

COVERING ALL BETS

WILLIAM WALTON is unique among coaches. Coaches have on occasions had to umpire matches in which their team was playing, but Walton must be the only man to ever play against a team he was coaching. This remarkable event actually happened twice in the VFA in 1922. Walton was appointed coach of Hawthorn but Port, for whom he had been playing, refused to clear him. A compromise was reached. He could coach Hawthorn during the week and play for Port, so he actually played twice against his own charges.

THE CLASSICISTS

Many coaches like to draw on history for anecdotes to get their message across.

Ex-North Melbourne icon, 'SLAMMIN' SAM' KEKOVICH, was in charge of a New South Wales team which played interstate games against Queensland and Tasmania.

The first game was against Queensland, and the New South Wales boys found themselves in Queensland on the eve of the game doing circuit work with only three footballs. It was hot and humid and a short run would have sufficed. Sam got a bit a carried away with his news conference however and forgot to tell the boys to stop. When the last cable had been wrapped, the boys were a sopping, sore-muscled mess.

By the end of the first quarter of the match next day, NSW led by about 5 goals. From there it was all uphill and they ended up beaten.

Next the team travelled to Tasmania where, before the game, Sam gave a stirring oration. He told his players about the Phoenicians and the Romans; how the Phoenicians had sailed to enemy territory, tried to defeat the Romans, copped a hiding and been forced to jump back in their ships and go home. Undeterred they had bided their time and sallied forth again. This time, they had burned the ships once they landed. This time, the Phoenicians had triumphed.

The plumbers and machinists who formed Sam's constituents were really more interested in which side of the ground they ought to be kicking to and who they were playing than on this ancient history lesson, but Sam soon made the parable clear to them.

He explained that they were just like the Phoenicians, there was no turning back.

NSW got beaten by about 6 goals.

Sam, after various official exchanges had been completed, was last on the coach, where his team had been patiently waiting.

Keko's head had barely appeared in the stairwell when one of the smart arses showed Sam his pre-game lecture had not been wasted.

'It's a good thing we didn't burn the coaches,' he shouted.

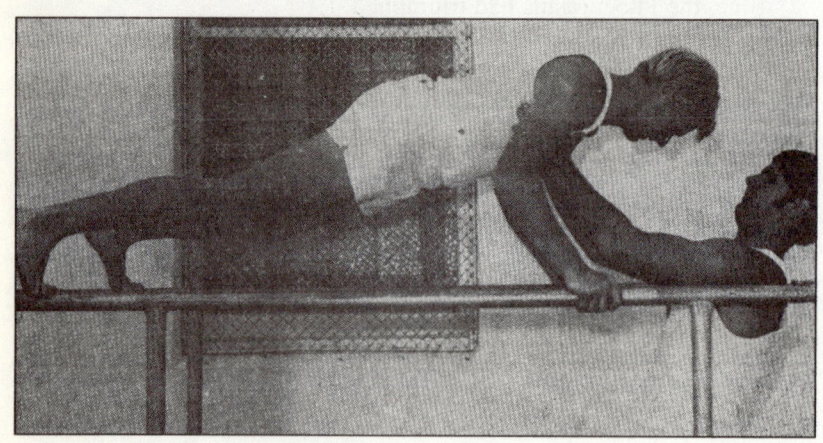

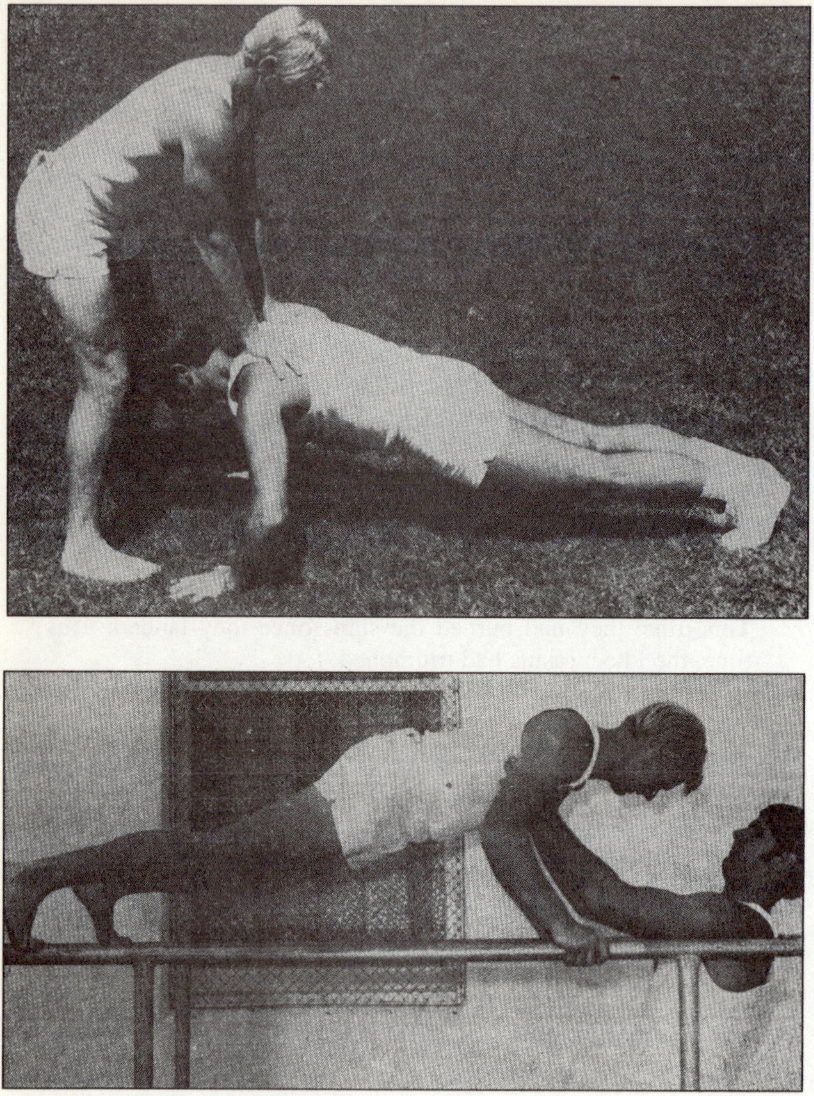

Dud coaching manual. (H P Mann.)

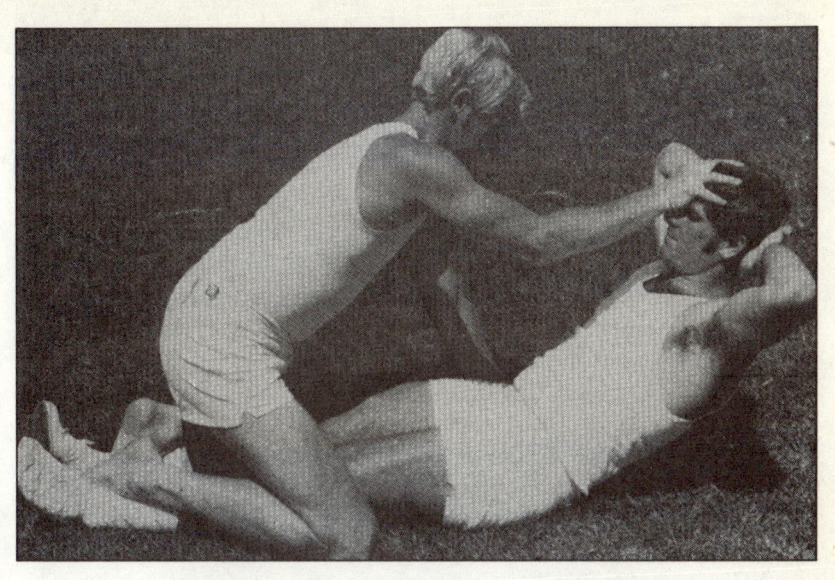

IAN RIDLEY, according to CRACKERS KEENAN, was another given to the parable. Crackers recounts a pre-match address by Ridley in which the great city of London was extolled.

It was 1971, Keenan's Melbourne and their opponents, Collingwood, were both coming off good winning runs. Ridley told his players they were like London: it had taken 2000 years to make London a great city but in 1940 it took just one day for Hitler to bomb the shit out of it. If the Poms had put their barrage balloons and fighters up there though, Hitler never would have got through. He concluded that there were a lot of bloody Hitlers next door, to which Keenan asided that he thought Ernie Hug might have been the only German.

As it happened, Collingwood did indeed blast Melbourne the way the Germans had ruined London. At the end of the match Crackers asked Lloyd Burgman, 'What are you going to do?'

He said, 'I dunno, I'm going down to Coles to buy some balloons.'

PENANCE

When former Hawthorn player BRIAN DOUGE was captain-coach of Subiaco he told his players before their game against South Fremantle down at the port, that he was going to 'take out' MAURICE RIOLI.

This was going to be something worth seeing. Douge was not normally the sort to whack a man and besides, Rioli was one of the best boxers in the game as Mark Jackson, among others, had discovered.

South's coach Mal Brown had gloveman Laurie Flanders at training sharpening the players' skills. Jackson didn't think that Maurice warranted the respect the other players seemed to have for Rioli and decided he would take him on and prove he was top cock in town.

Brown, obviously feeling that the brash young Victorian, given to dropping his daks on field, could do with a lesson, obliged

Jacko.

Jackson, who left the bout in no doubt of Maurice's clout.

Douge's players wondered whether he had heard this story? Perhaps things were tougher in the VFL than they imagined. Certainly the prospect of their coach leading from the front had them fired up.

But for all that pre-game enthusiasm, at half-time Rioli had carved them up, and some of the senior players had mentioned to Douge that perhaps now was the time to deliver on his threat.

'I've almost got him,' assured Douge.

The third quarter came and went, the margin increased and still the players waited. The last quarter came and the final siren sounded with South comprehensive winners and Rioli untouched.

Douge then punished himself for his failings, but not in quite the way his players had envisaged: he ran from Fremantle Oval all the way back to Subiaco (some 20 kms) for trophy presentations.

THE FLAG THAT GOT AWAY

PORT ADELAIDE'S officials might have stood by their principles, but in denying their team the opportunity to take the field in a premiership decider they deprived their players and fans of a flag and a place in the right pages of the history books.

After finishing on top of the ladder in 1902 Port forfeited its Semi-Final match to South. In the lead up to the match Port had written to the South Australian Football Association stating it would forfeit if umpire Phil Kneebone was appointed to control the game. Umpire Kneebone was appointed and Port were disqualified and placed third on the ladder.

ROD CARTER

When South Melbourne became the SYDNEY SWANS and relocated to the Harbour city, some players refused to move. As the years have gone by, other players have defected to Victorian clubs for the chance of success.

The Sydney Swans were really a brand-new club needing desperately to hook into some tradition of their own.

One player who personified club loyalty above individual honours was their full-back, Rod Carter.

After 76 games with Fitzroy, Carter had moved to the Swans in 1980 and played over 200 games in the red and white. Unfortunately 1990 was proving about as good a year for the Swans as 1945 was for the people of Nagasaki.

Carter was down on form too, though no more than the majority of his team-mates.

It was a complete bombshell then when the match committee dropped Carter just 7 games short of his 300. The fragile foundations of the club were rocked, putting Sydney as a club back a number of years.

At a time when the club desperately needed to reward loyalty it snubbed it.

When the Swans dumped John Northey as coach at the end of 1985 because he didn't have a high enough profile, it left a bitter taste in the mouths of many. Coaches, though, know that they will always be a likely scapegoat and as bad as it was, it paled in comparison to the shoddy treatment afforded Carter.

MICHAEL TUCK

Michael Tuck was revered at Hawthorn the way the Yanks revere their flag.

The holder of the record number of games had run out onto the ground 426 times to defend the honour of the gold and brown. He had slogged it out in hail and heat; he had run his legs the equivalent of a couple of laps of the nation. He had been prepared to play the majority of his footy in the shadow of Hawthorn's other stars; he was the personification of endurance and loyalty.

Then in 1992, after his retirement, Tuck covered the Hawthorn-Eagles final at Subiaco for a Melbourne paper and the unthinkable happened.

Hawthorn banned from their change rooms 'Father Time', Michael Tuck, and brought SHAME upon their house.

BLACK AND WHITE MINSTREL SHOW

ALAN McALISTER'S tenure as Collingwood president might best be described as 'colourful'. It was colour that kept getting Mac into trouble. First there were claims that Collingwood was a racist club. It didn't recruit Aboriginal players and it didn't protect Aboriginal players from rabid Collingwood supporters. McAlister's comments that Aborigines would be accepted if only they behaved themselves like white people caused a furore. The Pies' President claimed he had not meant to say what had come out of his mouth and, given his history of gaffes, this is probably true. Just imagine though if the white people that Aboriginal players emulated were some of the more extreme Collingwood supporters!

DOCTOR FEELBAD

Here are some instances where club doctors definitely inducted themselves into the Hall Of Shame.

CHRIS STASINOWSKY

CHRIS STASINOWSKY, who played in both WA and SA, was a talented but troubled player who tragically committed suicide.

On one occasion he was due to line up for West Perth in a very important match against East Perth but was concerned about some leg problems he was having and decided to consult a doctor. For some reason he did not go to the club doctor.

The GP whom he visited did a cursory examination and then gave 'Stazza' the bad news. The injury ought not be aggravated. He should at least miss the next match, failure to do so could invite drastic consequences.

Stasinowsky duly pulled out of the West Perth side, obviously unaware that the doctor whom he had consulted was East Perth's club doctor!

DAVID STIRLING (Sydney Swans) had big gaps between his teeth and chronic hamstring problems. The Swans' club doctor apparently believed the two related. He advised Stirling to have all his teeth out if he wanted to clear up the hammys. Stirling decided he'd rather keep his teeth.

GARTH DICKER

Fitzroy club doctor Garth Dicker must have been watching too much 'M.A.S.H.' His behaviour in the infamous Coogee Holiday Inn affair certainly owed more to Hawkeye than Hippocrates.

After Fitzroy's 1995 round 4 loss to the Swans in Sydney some of the Fitzroy players and officials decided to check their brains into reception instead of their bags.

At the AFL-patronised Coogee Holiday Inn, property was destroyed, food thrown and staff harassed. It was like something out of *Animal House*.

The aftermath: Jason Baldwin stripped of his vice-captaincy, suspended for 2 matches and fined $5000; Nick Mitchell suspended for 1 match, fined $2,000 and ordered to pay $800 for damages; Dicker fined $10,000 for disturbances in the breakfast area.

DON'T SHOOT THE MESSENGER
RUNNERS' TALES

Runners have an unenviable task when angry coaches send them out to confront players and umpires. Often, too, runners are literally run into the ground! Mind you, runners are pretty adept at dodging the coaches' worst demands. Here are some instances in which the coach, the runner or both have inducted themselves into the Hall Of Shame.

EVASIVE ACTION

JIM SEWELL (East Fremantle, Footscray) found himself acting as MAL BROWN'S runner in a State game. When the umpire made a series of decisions with which Browny disagreed he sent Sewell to tell the umpire he was a useless piece of ##%and!!.

'And I'll know whether or not you do it,' thundered the omniscient Brown down the phone.

Sewell ran to the umpire and told him the coach had said he was a useless piece of ##%and!!.

The umpire cooly told Sewell that he would disregard that message but that any repetition would result in both him and his coach going into the book on abusive language charges.

Sewell got back to the dugout and relayed this to Brown. Things went pretty well from there until late in the game when the umpire again awarded a dubious free kick against WA, resulting in a goal. Sewell didn't have to wait long for the phone to buzz.

'Go out there and tell that useless piece of ###and%$ that he's a useless piece of **%#!!,' yelled Brown.

'You know what he said?' Sewell was trying to temper an enraged bull and knew he had no chance.

'I know what he said and I don't care. Get out there,' ordered the coach.

Sewell ran towards the umpire who had been waiting for the missive. The umpire paused with the ball in his hand, not prepared to bounce it until the message which he knew was coming had arrived. A panting Sewell reached the centre square.

'Ump,' said Sewell, 'he said it again.'

NO SKIN OFF MY NOSE

Playing in the 2s against Footscray, St Kilda's **ROBBIE MUIR** had been free-kicked in the centre and then, for failure to come back on the mark, had been given a series of penalties down to the goal square where Footscray had duly goaled. Everybody on the ground sensed Robbie was about to explode. Obviously the Saints' bench knew it too. The runner ran out onto the ground.

'Come off, Robbie, time to come off,' he yelled from some 30 metres away.

Muir glowered back and the runner retreated. At the next bounce down Albie Smedts felt the full fury of Muir's displeasure.

Muir received 8 weeks for kicking.

THE WOLF IN BO PEEP

ROBERT WILEY goes into the Runner's Hall Of Shame for getting himself reported in his first game as a runner. Wiley had played around 300 games with the malice of Bo Peep and consequently had never been reported.

But when he saw Eagle Murray Rance in trouble on the boundary line, he forgot his new job and joined in the affray.

Poor Gary Bygraves. During his playing days the bow-legged Bygraves was nicknamed 'Cowboy'.

Whether his tastes were quite as gourmet as St Kilda's identically named 'Cowboy' Kevin Neale is unknown, but certainly, when Bygraves fronted for his first game as a runner for former team East Perth in 1989, he was in better post-retirement shape than the former St Kilda full-forward.

In fact, he wasn't far off his playing weight before the game against East Fremantle, and after it he weighed less than Kate Moss.

Whether Bygraves was simply unable to remember the messages of former team-mate and debutant coach Ian McCullough, or whether McCullough kept changing his mind, couldn't be determined from the other side of the boundary line, but Bygraves spent more time on the ground than the grass. He covered twice as much territory as Mao in his long march.

Finally, a bedraggled, ruddy Bygraves cramped up and had to be replaced ... in the third quarter!

CRAIG HOLDEN

In 1995 Tony Lockett kicked a record 16 goals for the Swans but he could have broken Fred Fanning's long-standing record of 18 goals had communication with runner Craig Holden been a little better.

Lockett, with 10 goals to date, spent 12 minutes on the bench in the second quarter after Holden came out and told him to 'cool it' following the big fellow's clash with Mark Zanotti.

Somehow Lockett thought the command was 'come off'.

The match committee thought Lockett was off under the 'blood' rule.

In lieu of a stretch in the Hall Of Shame we sentence Craig Holden to an elocution course.

TRAINERS' INACTION

GONE TO THE DOGS

From 1975 to 1984 Subiaco won just 53 of 210 games. In 1982 they won just 1. During this time, morale hit an all-time low, best illustrated by the following tale.

A Subi player received a heavy knock and was face-down on the ground when reached by a trainer. The trainer turned the player over with his foot, indicated a stretcher was needed, then left the scene, hurdling the fence to buy a hot dog.

In 1967, Subi's Russell Watkins was wiped out 15 metres from the boundary line. The trainer acted quickly, running to Watkins and dragging him from the arena by the ankles.

It was also a Subiaco trainer, Barry Windsor, whose corpulent frame was propelled over the fence by East Fremantle rover David Bushell when he strayed into Bushell's path. Bushell received a suspension.

Adelaide's trainer GARY GOUDGE had to be elbowed out of the way by his own player Tony McGuinness as McGuinness ran at the ball.

Dud duds.
(Sporting Pix.)

60

BOTTOM OF THE LOCKER

AN ASSORTMENT OF THE DUBIOUS AND DEVIOUS

CRUD DUDS
THE WORST GEAR WORN ON A FOOTY FIELD

TEAM UNIFORMS

When the BRISBANE BEARS made their debut in 1987, the Dow Jones was still rising and the love of all things corporate imbued board members from Parliament to footy clubs. This is why the Brisbane Bears took the field with a guernsey that looked like a logo for a life insurance company. The numbers on the backs of the jumpers were underlined too, presumably so we could tell 6 from 9 as the player tumbled from the top of the pack. Unfortunately the only thing that tumbled was the Dow, dragging the fledgling Bears back faster than a speculative mineral. Subsequent Bears' efforts, featuring maps of Queensland and bear heads, had more place in front of a barrage of Japanese tourists' flashes than a rushing pack of demented AFL opponents. The club finally got the message and with a traditional club structure and guernsey design started to put all that Teddy Bear picnic back in its corporate box where it belonged.

WAFL club SUBIACO went through a period of new coaches and guernseys in the late-'70s Their azimuth of design defect was an all-gold strip with heraldic lion. One expected the players to morris dance on the Members wing, or at least chase a greased piglet. In fact the way they handled the ball, they might have had more luck with a greased piglet.

Some other appalling apparel foisted on players includes ESSENDON'S red shorts strip and the 'ALLIES' outfit that makes its players look like assistants in an ice-cream parlour.

At the time of writing the worst strip in the AFL is clearly the CROWS oppressive primary-coloured hoops that make its players look like squashed licorice allsorts.

Into the Hall Of Shame for their fashion accessorising must go the following players:

TONY CAMPBELL (Melbourne and Footscray, 1986-93) has etched his name into the Hall Of Shame for introducing GLOVES into football. In combination with his slicked hair, these gloves made the corpulent full-back look like a commissionaire for a Wall Street apartment block.

Much more acceptable were DERMOTT BRERETON'S GREEN BOOTS although they should have remained a St Pat's Day special — an implement for drinking green beer from.

BARRY CABLE was already striking enough with his blond hair and amazing skill but then, in a case of overkill, he went and added white sockettes! Cable got the ball so often and moved so fast, it made anybody watching the game feel like they were running beside a white picket fence.

SAM NEWMAN and WARWICK CAPPER went the white boots which, given their strip, was at least colour coordinated.

Capper, of course, was the master of the tight shorts, a fashion statement that had its devotees able to make a living doing Bee Gees' impersonations even if they didn't make it as footballers.

John Todd showing some flare. (West Australian.)

THE WORST MASCOT

No contest here, the SYDNEY SWANS' giant Swan wins it wings down. With its long, long neck and its wobbling fat torso the Swan was an embarrassment to players and fans.

On one occasion at the last break in a close game, Swans' coach Ricky Quade was trying to impress on his players the importance of winning the game and how to go about it. He was totally lost for words when that stupid swan craned its long stupid neck over the phalanx of players and into the huddle.

Even more embarrassing for the players was the time they had to run through a banner congratulating the Swan on its 50th appearance. True, a 50th appearance was a rare milestone for anybody in Sydney's colours those days, but even so, having to run through a banner for a mascot — and a dumb-looking mascot at that — was just too SHAMEFUL.

The CROWS' secondary mascot, the Camry chicken, has great potential to emulate the Swan.

(Photo: Tony Nolan.)

HQ-POQs
THE WORST OVALS AND GROUND STAFF SKULDUGGERY

What are the worst ovals league football has been played on? What are the worst grounds for fans to watch a game? What are the sneakiest tricks played by ground staff to give the home team an advantage? Here are our nominations.

The muddy surface of HAWTHORN'S old home ground Glenferrie made it more like a piggery than a footy oval, but at least they didn't play finals there. As any footy fan who has ever travelled to the ice belt of Melbourne called WAVERLY can testify, the AFL-built headquarters is without doubt the costliest piece of torture ever foisted on the Aussie Rules footy fan. When the skies over the rest of Melbourne sparkle like a polished sapphire, those by Waverly are battleship grey. While the crickets sing a cheerful tune in the still Melbourne air of other grounds, the wind at Waverly howls like a starved hound. When it rains in Melbourne's inner suburbs, it hails at Waverly.

At least the AFL can make some money from the government. It's hard to imagine a better training ground for the SAS than the cold, foreboding bowels of Waverly. What chance would a terrorist group have against troops forced to endure a Waverly sleetfest from the exposed outer!

AND FOR SPECIFICS

WAVERLY PARK, 1993: FOSTERS CUP

What a monumental stuff-up this was. Are we sure it was the Brits who were responsible for Gallipoli and not Barry Capuano and the AFL? In the 1993 pre-season competition big chunks of turf flew out of the ground as players ran for the ball in a Footscray-Carlton game. Dogs' coach Terry Wheeler considered going to his rival David Parkin and saying, 'Let's call the whole thing off.' Luke O'Sullivan wished he had. The Blue's forward did a knee that put him out for the season.

Capuano had resigned as operations manager within a couple of weeks.

CLAREMONT OVAL

When Claremont's grandstand burned down in 1944 and the playing surface went to ruin, the Tigers were forced to switch to Subiaco Oval for games (1945-47). In 1947 the council promised 'change sheds' for players so Claremont could train there — but these sheds were actually disued army huts. For nearly 10 years these sheds were the 'facilities' for both home and away teams at Claremont. Supporters and opposition clubs could clearly hear what coaches were saying in their address, as the players were forced to sit on earthern floors.

Another shameful episode in Claremont's history came in 1948 when they had to call over the loudspeaker for eligible players to make up their teams.

MOORABBIN MORASS

From the mid-'70s to '80s ST KILDA languished on or near the bottom of the table and the Saints' home games had more resemblance to mud wrestling than a footy match. Sometimes, even when it hadn't rained for weeks, Morabbin contained more mud than a Joan Collins face-pack. The mystery was solved years later when a retiring head groundsman admitted that under the coach's (Tony Jewel among others) instructions, he had watered the ground to bring the opposition clubs back to the Saints' level!

In 1981 the Western Australian club side CLAREMONT were playing against champion VFL side HAWTHORN in an Escort Cup night match at Waverly Park. With players like the Krakouer brothers and Ken Hunter in their side, the 'Monts were doing very well on the firm, fast surface of Waverly. Jim Krakouer was lining up for a shot on goal when the sprinklers suddenly came on soaking the ground! With the slippery ball and soggy ground Claremont's skills evaporated. Hawthorn won and declined Claremont's invitation of a replay.

ALL TIME WORST PROMOTIONS

Football clubs and bodies seem to love the idea of the Big Promotion. No doubt the insane desire to turn footy and footy games into some sort of antipodean Disneyland has its genesis in 'fact-finding sports junkets'. Feeling warm and fuzzy from all the complimentary Jack Daniels, the sports supremos attend the Superbowl and come back drooling at the spectacular entertainment the Yanks have on tap. Flush with the spirit, our captains of leisure return unsteadily to these shores and begin a master plan to take our game to the world or bring the world to our game.

Here are some of the more grandiose or bizarre efforts that deserve a place in the Hall Of Shame.

Canada seems to be a favourite place to stage Aussie Rules fiascos. Obviously somebody has a girlfriend over there, otherwise what on earth were WA and SA doing in October 1988 playing a game between two below-strength line-ups? That 1800 people turned up to see WA win 18.14 to 17.13 is amazing; even if all the tickets were given away.

Another stroke of genius was the time the SWANS played MELBOURNE in Vancouver. The winner got to hang around Vancouver to play a decider against the winners of a game played in London. The losers got a leave pass for a week with the only proviso being that they turn up at LA airport to get the flight back. With the chance of a week travelling the USA while being paid an expense allowance, what would you do?

The image of JOHN IRONMONGER chewing into raw-meat to promote the game to our Canadian friends as something only vicious and moronic thugs would partake of, is also up there as inspired promo. For John's sake we just hope he doesn't come down with Mad Cow, Hep C or any of the other wonderful maladies such a stunt could bring.

CONVERTING THE HEATHEN

Another great attempt to champion Aussie Rules in the very temple of the unbelievers, came when the SYDNEY SWANS first moved to Sydney. It was somebody's brilliant idea to have the Swans do circuit work during the lunchbreak of the New Year's Test. Every time a Swan went near the boundary line he was pelted with rubbish and annointed with such terms of endearment as 'faggot' 'fairy' and 'woos'.

The SCG was again Venue Of Shame when a wedding ceremony was performed at half-time during a Sydney Swans' match. As the wags in the crowd observed, just down the player's race was an unlimited supply of bridesmaids.

The cringe meter ran hot ran when the VFL decided that Peter Allen in a pink jumpsuit was appropriate pre-game entertainment for the COLLINGWOOD V RICHMOND 1980 Grand Final. The sort of Vegas pizzazz that was Allen's specialty had the crowd hooting and howling derisively. It wasn't that Allen was a bad act, just that there was hardly a less appropriate act for an MCG opener in the entire world.

Conversely, the Grand Final celebration in which the entire MCG became a sea of goal umpires was spot-on. Sure it was quaint, bizarre, even surreal, but it was ultimately so suburban, so bodgy, so unpolished that it became a triumph.

Many deep thinkers were seen to nod all-knowingly to themselves at the spectacle of goal umpires each moving to the beat of their own drum, hopelessly out of sync with any other. Wasn't this a great philosophical statement by the AFL — that we each have goals and that we each must pursue them however we can? Didn't this say that Aussie Rules is not a precise sport, not a game for the subjugation of, but rather the celebration of the individual? Tacky it may have been, but in all its glorious slapdashedness the goal umpire act became a sublime apex in event management.

Who was the marketing guru who thought this one up?

In a soft drink promotion Eagle DEAN KEMP was forced to humiliate himself in front of thousands of fans at the WAFL 1993 Grand Final by leading a hovering helicopter nicknamed MAX around the oval while an innane commentary was made as if Max was a pet ('Come here Max, good boy Max').

What was the message they were trying to get across? Drink this product to look like a complete dork?

As the chopper flew off and Dean Kemp sank in relief, thousands of fans gave it the bird. The pilot obviously mistook this mark of derision for some sort of compliment and flew back again to only redouble the crowd's jeering.

TURLEY MASK

Oh yes, this was a beauty. The radio station idea was to have a sea of faces of the Eagle's pin-up boy CRAIG TURLEY. The Eagles themselves weren't too rapt in the idea of having one player singled out thus and made a poisoned-pill offer: the promotion could go ahead if the face of PETER WILSON was used.

As Willo's visage was such to crack glass, the idea was hastily abandoned.

The rules on the back of the mask — known as THE ORIGINAL FOOTY FAN — read as if written by a graduate of the *Hey Dad* school of humour.

WAVE THE ORIGINAL FOOTY FAN

1. When an Eagle kicks a goal. (This is compulsory.)
2. When an Eagle takes a mark. (This is almost as compulsory as 1.)
3. When the Umpire, quite fairly, justly and appropriately awards the Eagles a free kick.

4. When the Umpire blows it.
5. When the umpire trips over his guide dog and misses a free kick that Ray Charles could have seen.
6. When an opposition player 'spits the dummy'. (Expect this to happen often.)
7. When an opposition supporter begins to open his or her mouth.
8. When a player loses his shorts, the Original Footy Fan should be raised to avoid player embarrassment. (Female fans are exempt from this rule and may use binoculars.)
9. When the Goal Umpire indicates with his fingers exactly how big it is.

(10th rule deleted as it is a promotional blurb.)

Chip 'n' Dale gathering nuts. (Christo/Fairfax Photo Library.)

THE DISHONOUR BOARD

THE WORST OF THE WORST

Being a successful club is great. But it is, after all, what clubs set out to do. What would appear to require far more talent is to be hugely unsuccessful despite every effort not to be.

Or maybe it is all down to portents? Perhaps success is more about choosing the right name for your club than the right players? Certainly any embryonic clubs contemplating a name starting with S should beware. The three dudliest clubs in the three main comps are Subiaco, South Adelaide and St Kilda. Pressing them close are Swan Districts, Sturt and South Melbourne/Sydney Swans. Talk about giving you the 's's'.

Just have a gander at the damage these clubs have made to the trophy cabinet business.

MAROONED

During their history SUBIACO have proven themselves the footstool of the WAFL competition. Prior to their current good run that began in the mid-1980s Subiaco were to football what the Leyland P76 was to the Aussie auto industry.

Just a snapshot of their WAFL lowlights reveals:

- Most years without a premiership (48 years: 1925-72)
- Longest sequence of losses (29: 1901-03)
- Most wooden spoons (19).

AND THERE'S MORE!!!! The 1906 Maroons managed to go through an entire game without scoring. They're the only 20th century club to do that in three main comps.

Subi were the opponents the day South Fremantle's Bernie Naylor kicked 23 goals in a game and 12 goals in one quarter.

In addition to their on-field flops, they came out with one of the silliest guernsey designs of all time — the yellow heraldic strip that had them nicknamed 'The Canaries'.

Across the rabbit-proof from Subiaco, SOUTH ADELAIDE have come to be synonymous with subterranean success.

To be fair, they are more enigmatic than inept, having gone from last in 1963 to win the 1964 flag. That was only their third this century and they haven't won one since.

In fact most of South's silverware is pre-Federation when they were one of the only clubs going round.

The club has so many wooden spoons it is probably responsible for a large tract of lost Amazonian rainforest. The loss-win ration is a staggering 63%, which probably matches the proof on the bottles their supporters need to guzzle to keep from contemplating reality.

And look at their premiership droughts! Flagless between 1900 and 1934, and again since 1964. Disco, flares, punk rock and Kamahl have all come and gone since that last flag. The Beatles have come, gone and come back again.

South have some lovely winless streaks too.

But they had better not get complacent. STURT are making a withering run with a record 7 consecutive wooden spoons; 1989-95 inclusive. Coming off a year in which they had not a single win, Sturt are looking like they could go all the way and spend a whole decade on the bottom of the ladder.

For the masochists, a more complete lowdown on both South and Sturt appears in CLUB DUD.

... AND BOTTOM AT THE HARBOUR

SOUTH MELBOURNE/ SYDNEY SWANS have a couple of things going for them in the quest for haplessness: they haven't been in a Grand Final for 50 years, haven't won a flag in more than 60 years (the longest current drought among clubs) and have not 1, but 2 fabulous losing streaks: 29 (1972-3) and 26 (1992-3).

But for all the accomplishments of the Swans, Subiaco and South Adelaide there can be no dispute that ST KILDA are in a class of their own when it comes to incompetence. Consider these Lilliputian efforts:

• A solitary premiership in their 99-year history — and that by the lowest possible margin: 1 point!
• Most wooden spoons (25) of any club in the 3 main comps, including a peerless 5 times going through a season winless. Longest premiership drought (69 yrs) 1897–1965.
• A VFL record low score of 0.1 (v Geelong, 1899) and several other shockers (*see CLUB DUD section*), with the modern-day Saints harking back to their predecessors with scores of 1.5 (v Melbourne, 1957) and 3.18 (v West Coast, 1988).
• Admissions by the grounds people that the quagmire which was Moorabbin Oval, was made by them conducting secret watering on instructions from coaching staff.
• Two of the classic bad trades of all time — Ian Stewart to Richmond in exchange for Bill Barrot, and Russell Greene to Hawthorn.
• A shocking logo: a stick man with a basketball hoop on his head.

All in all, St Kilda have the bottom of the footy locker to themselves. Which is not to say we don't love them.

When US sports buffs talk about the endearing incompetence of the Atlanta Falcons or the 1962 New York Mets we know that they have nothing on the Saints.

Long live the Saints and all the other under performers in our great game. They're much more fun to talk about than those boring winning machines.

See CLUB DUD for a full rundown of the Saints' remarkable achievements.

BIG DROUGHTS

For taking so long to reward their supporters these clubs are inducted into the Hall Of Shame.

THE LONGEST PREMIERSHIP DROUGHTS IN FOOTY HISTORY

ST KILDA	69 yrs	1897-1965
SOUTH MELB/SYDNEY	62	1934-1995
FITZROY	51	1945-1995
NORTH MELBOURNE	50	1925-1974
SUBIACO	48	1925-1972
PERTH	47	1908-1954
FOOTSCRAY	41	1955-1995
GLENELG *	38	1935-1972
WEST TORRENS	37	1954-1990

*There was no competition in SA from 1942-44 inclusive so Glenelg's effort by season isn't quite as bad as it looks.

The longest time it has taken a club to win its first premiership is another St Kilda record, though Central Districts haven't managed one yet. Interestingly a club's 27th season seems to be when it clicks. Three clubs graduated to premiers in the 27th season of competition.

ST KILDA	69 yrs	1897-1965
NORTH MELBOURNE	50	1925-1974
CENTRAL DISTRICTS*	32	1964-1995
HAWTHORN	36	1925-1960
FOOTSCRAY	29	1925-1953
WOODVILLE^	27	1964-1990
SWAN DISTRICTS	27	1934-1960
GEELONG #	27	1897-1924

* no premiership to date.
^ did not win a premiership as Woodville only as Woodville-West Torrens.
# did not compete 1916.

Currently longest without flags and thereby inducted into the Hall Of Shame.

LEAST SUCCESSFUL CLUBS

BY RATIO: FLAGS DIVIDED BY YEARS IN COMPETITION

(by clubs with 15 years or more in comp)

If you take the average Australian lifespan and compare it to these tables you could be in for a shock. The chances are if you're a St Kilda fan, you'll die before they win a premiership! Footscray fans, you might just scrape in with good health care.

As in above stats, Woodville and West Torrens figures do not allow for Woodville-West Torrens merger flags to be counted.

FLAGS PER YEAR IN COMPETITION

	NUMBER OF FLAGS	AVG WAIT BY SEASONS
CENTRAL DISTRICTS	0	—
WOODVILLE	0	—
ST KILDA	1	97
FOOTSCRAY	1	71
NORTH MELBOURNE	2	35
SOUTH MELB/SYDNEY	3	32
WEST TORRENS	4	23
GLENELG	4	16
GEELONG	6	16

MOST FREQUENT WOODEN SPOONERS BY RATIO OF SPOONS TO YEARS IN COMPETITION

For once a statistic that doesn't point to the Saints as the most hopeless club in the land! That dubious honour going to the defunct Woodpeckers.

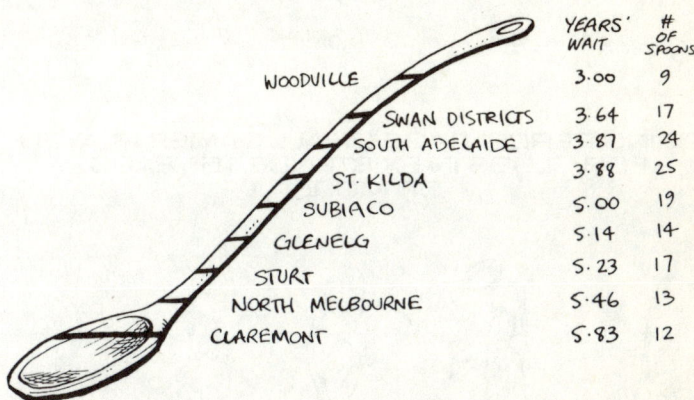

	YEARS' WAIT	# OF SPOONS
WOODVILLE	3.00	9
SWAN DISTRICTS	3.64	17
SOUTH ADELAIDE	3.87	24
ST. KILDA	3.88	25
SUBIACO	5.00	19
GLENELG	5.14	14
STURT	5.23	17
NORTH MELBOURNE	5.46	13
CLAREMONT	5.83	12

THE GREATEST WINLESS STREAKS

0 WINS IN A SEASON
(CLUBS STILL EXISTING AUTONOMOUSLY OR THROUGH AMALGAMATION)

5 TIMES   4 TIMES   3 TIMES   2 TIMES

LOSING PERCENTAGE OF ALL GAMES PLAYED FOR CLUBS IN EXISTENCE 15 YEARS OR MORE

55%
GLENELG
CENTRALS
SYDNEY / STH. MELB.
FOOTSCRAY

58%
SUBIACO
NTH. MELB.

60%
SWAN
DISTRICTS

63%
ST. KILDA
STH. ADELAIDE

71%
WOODVILLE

(NB. SANFL stats from 1907.)

HOW LOW CAN YOU GO?

THE GREATEST THRASHINGS IN FOOTY HISTORY

Most teams can't kick 170 points let alone LOSE by that margin. But here you go, the table below shows the greatest pants-down thrashings handed out in footy history. South Fremantle's 1944 team was at least part of a wartime under-age competition, but what on earth were those Central Districts players up to back in 1975? Maybe they were listening to Bob Dylan and the Eagles and smoking funny stuff? They were certainly Taking It Easy while Glenelg were Doing It Easy. Nice to see our friends South Adelaide in the thick of things in most decades with entries in 1959, 1972 and 1988 — I guess you could call them 'recidivist'.

MARGIN OF DEFEAT	LOSER	YEAR
256	S Ftle to E Pth	1944
238	Centrals to Glenelg	1975
198	Torrens to Centrals	1988
192	Subiaco to S Ftle	1953
190	Melb to Fitzroy	1979
180	West Perth to S Ftle	1981
178	S Adel to North	1972
178	S Adel to Centrals	1988
178	St Kilda to Collwd	1978
178	E Ftle to W Pth	1981
175	S Adel to W Adel	1959
173	Perth to Clmnt	1981
171	St Kilda to S Mel	1919

THE LOWEST LOSING SCORES

PRE-WORLD WAR 2
These are self-explanatory. They reveal the early West Adelaide and St Kilda teams to have been extremely scoreboard attendant friendly. Not only did those teams usually not win ANY games in a season, they barely scored at all.

West Adel	0.0	v Norwood	1897
West Adel	0.0	v North Adel	1897
Subiaco	0.0	v South Ftle	1906
St Kilda	0.1	v Geelong	1899
Perth	0.1	v West Perth	1899
West Adel	0.1	v Port Adel	1899
West Adel	0.2	v South Adel	1898
St Kilda	0.2	v South Mel	1897
East Ftle	0.2	v Rovers	1898
West Adel	0.3	v Port Adel	1904
West Perth	0.3	v Subiaco	1912
Perth	0.3	v East Ftle	1903
St Kilda	0.3	v Essendon	1897

POST-WORLD WAR 2

The surprise here is the West Coast Eagles 1989 effort against Essendon. Dealt with elsewhere in this book, it remains an absolute stand-out lowlight in any category. Richmond's goalless 1961 effort against St Kilda looks like it has come from a century before. As the table shows, any side playing Port Adelaide has to be wary of being added to the low-score humiliated. They are so efficient at putting on the tighteners they make Peter Walsh look like Santa Claus.

Fitzroy	1. 0	v Footscray	1953
Richmond	0. 8	v St Kilda	1961
Claremont	1. 3	v Perth	1945
South Adel	1. 4	v Sturt	1973
East Perth	1. 4	v Perth	1956
Subiaco	1. 5	v East Ftle	1954
Central Dist	1. 6	v Port Adel	1967
Perth	1. 7	v Sth Ftle	1952
Footscray	1. 8	v Geelong	1965
W C Eagles	1.12	v Essendon	1989
West Adel	2. 2	v Port Adel	1968
North Adel	1. 8	v Port Adel	1989 G.Final
Brisbane	2. 5	v Hawthorn	1988
Central Dist	2. 5	v Port Adel	1964
Woodville	2. 5	v Port Adel	1967
Norwood	2. 5	v Port Adel	1988 2nd Semi

LOWEST AGGREGATE TOTALS FOR A MATCH

It is reported (not confirmed) that a scoreless tie was recorded in Queensland in 1928. In a Grand Final of the Riana Association in Queensland in 1939 neither side scored a goal. Riana beat Nalone 0.8 to 0.4.

For some other mind-deadening contests check the table below. Can you imagine if you just looked down to put the sauce on the pie when one of the goals were scored?

14 pts	West Adel 1.1 tied West Torrens 1.1	1897
15 pts	Port Adel 1.4 d Norwood 0. 5	1909
16 pts	Sth Ftle 2.2 d Nth Ftle 0.2	1906
22 pts	Essendon 1.8 d Melbourne 0. 8	1897
23 pts	West Adel 1.8 d Nth Adel 1.3	1899
25 pts	Geelong 1.9 d Melbourne 0.10	1897
28 pts	East Perth 2.8 d Subiaco 1.2	1920
28 pts	Perth 2.5 d Nth Ftle 1.5	1904

MODERN DAY

What about Claremont and West Perth in 1950: did they think the country was still on rationing? The goal umpires had to do so little they probably put on weight during the game. And so much for the swinging sixties; there'd be more action at a lepidopterists slide night than the matches listed below.

50 pts	Port Adel 5.6 d West Adel 2.2	1968
53 pts	Glenelg 4.8 d Torrens 2.9	1957
56 pts	West Perth 5.4 d Perth 3.4	1964
57 pts	Claremont 3.13 v West Perth 3.8	1950
66 pts	West Perth 4.17 v Subiaco 3.3	1966
68 pts	North Mel 5.12 d Rich 3.8	1960
68 pts	East Ftle 6.10 West Perth 3.4	1964
68 pts	North Ad 5.11 d Wood-West Torr 3.9	1995
70 pts	East Perth 4.13 v Claremont 4.9	1966
70 pts	Subiaco 6.7 v East Ftle 3.9	1988
82 pts	West Coast 7.11 d Footscray 3.11	1988

THE 1927 VFL GRAND FINAL
COLLINGWOOD V RICHMOND

No chapter on low match aggregates would be complete without reference to this amazing non-spectacle.

Can you imagine a team could win a flag after not scoring a goal in the entire second half? In the conditions that transpired on the Big Day of 1927, the great Aussie swimmer Boy Charlton would have been more at home than the poor players who were forced to try and play footy.

The week had been wetter than the gags on 'Hey Dad', Melbourne was flooded and the MCG was a pond.

It was still bucketing down when the game started. Richmond's captain Geddes won the toss and pointed through sleet to the goals he hoped would be favoured.

After a mudfest the quarter time scores were Richmond 4 points, Collingwood 1 point.

When the rain became even heavier, Pies' coach Jock McHale told his players to soccer the ball, it being too slippery and heavy to control.

Collingwood's Gordon Coventry somehow took a chest mark and goaled and then followed-up 10 minutes later with a snap. It was to be the Pies' last goal, but it was still enough.

At half-time they led 2.6 to 0.4 — Richmond failing to score at all in the second quarter. Collingwood ran out winners 2.13 to 1.7

Norm Goss
South Melbourne
Rover

Worst footy swap card.

FINALS FLOPS AND FADE-OUTS

WORST FINALS PERFORMANCE

Some clubs are good at making finals and some clubs are good at winning them. Some clubs have nerves of steel, some have feet of clay. For a glimpse at the biggest heartbreakers, check the following tables.

THE WORST GRAND FINALISTS

The amazing thing here is that virtually all our dud clubs in general games are just as dud when it comes to finals. Look at Centrals — 1 Grand Final only, which they lost; St Kilda 4 Grand Finals of which they have lost 3, South Melbourne/ Sydney — 11 Grand Finals of which they have lost 8. Only Swan Districts (7 wins 2 losses) turn their normal persona on its head come Grand Final day. South Adelaide aren't that good, but they are good enough to miss this premiership putty crowd. It's no surprise that Collingwood are amongst the flag feeble.

No doubt about it though, the absolute Grand Final Pants-Down-Whip-Me-Cause-I-Deserve-It-Dills are Glenelg: 16 tries for 4 flags. Even Eddy The Eagle would be a better prospect. The fact that Glenelg don't even appear on our Worst Finals (overall) table shows that they get Big Day frights. They can win their way there but the only flag they own is a white one.

	Grand Finals PLAYED IN	% LOST
CENTRAL DISTRICTS	1	100
GLENELG	16	75
ST KILDA	4	75
SOUTH MEL/SYDNEY	11	73
NORTH MELBOURNE	6	66
COLLINGWOOD	36	61

SUBIACO	17	59
PERTH	17	59
GEELONG	14	57

THE WORST OVERALL FINALISTS

Leaving aside newcomers Brisbane, the finals dunces would appear to be the BULLDUDS. Centrals have lost an amazing 16 out of 20 finals matches and Footscray haven't proved much better. Before their merger both Torrens and Woodville were members of the finals-flops fraternity, Torrens shading the Peckers.

By percentage of finals played in, these are the worst finals performers. Not surprisingly most of our usual underachievers are here again.

	FINALS PLAYED IN	% LOST
BRISBANE	1	100
CENTRAL DISTRICTS	20	75
FOOTSCRAY	26	69
ADELAIDE	3	67
TORRENS	50	65
SOUTH ADELAIDE	40	62
ST KILDA	30	60
SOUTH MEL/SYDNEY	45	60
WOODVILLE	5	60

BIGGEST GRAND FINAL UPSETS

Some Grand Finals remind you of the Julia Roberts–Lyall Lovett wedding; a total mismatch. The coaches of the outsiders always say things like — 'if you're in the contest you can win it.' And most of us smugly say 'sure'.

Yet just occasionally that sentiment is proved true. Here are some instances where raging hot, unbackable, stone-bonker favourites got done.

EAST PERTH V SWAN DISTRICTS 1961

In the 1961 WAFL Grand Final East Perth were long odds-on to defeat Swan Districts.

Swans were new kids on the block, only ever once before appearing in a Grand Final some 18 years previously. What's more the Royals had beaten Swans 18 out of their last 19 clashes, including 4 times already that year, and by 8 goals in the Second Semi. East Perth was a team of tough hard veterans with a couple of Sandover Medallists and a number of state players on board. Swan Districts was a bunch of youngsters with a young coach, Haydn Bunton Jnr.

The match-up was like Wally Masur trying to take on Rod Laver.

Yet Swans, under coach Haydn Bunton Jnr triumphed 17.9 to 12.15 in the first of a trio of flags.

If the commentators, fans and critics reckoned that was the exception that proved the rule, they were dead wrong.

EAST FREMANTLE V CLAREMONT 1964

Three years later in the 1964 decider, East Fremantle were at almost the same odds as the Royals had been 3 years previously.

Grand Final upset of another kind. Bruce Doull and streaker, 1992, Carlton against Richmond. (Gary Lewis/Sporting Pix.)

Claremont, East Fremantle's opponent was a pre-season 20/1 outsider that had snuck into the final 4 like a self-conscious fourteen-year-old into a skin flick.

Any moment it seemed the big usher would come down and boot them blinking back into reality.

It was more than 20 years since the Tigers had played in the big one and even they seemed to have trouble believing they should be there!

But that year the Claremont Tigers had more luck than a Royal Commission witness at the races.

They made the final 4 in the last moments of the last qualifying game, then beat Subiaco by 12 points in the First Semi and Perth by 9 points in the Preliminary.

In a tremendous Grand Final, their Victorian recruit Ian Brewer kicked 2 deep pocket goals in the closing minutes while his opponent, Norm Rogers was receiving treatment for cramp.

The Claremont fans went crazy, hoisting their deckchairs in

the air and breasting the bars to order extra strong shandies before burning the lamps until well after 9.00 pm.

MELBOURNE V COLLINGWOOD 1958

By 1958 Norm Smith's Melbourne team had won 3 consecutive flags and stamped themselves as one of the all-time great combinations. With Ron Barassi firing the engine-room, that season they had beaten Collingwood in a Queen's Birthday game before 99,346 people and again in the Second Semi-Final. In the latter game the Pies had managed only 4 goals to the Demons' 12.

Though Collingwood were untroubled to beat North in the Preliminary and work their way for another crack at Melbourne, nobody except the most ardent Pies' fans gave them a chance.

Collingwood had managed only 1 drawn game with their rivals since 1955 and simply appeared to be outclassed.

It seemed like those World Championship Wrestling bouts where Con Tolios had to take on Killer Carl Cox.

Pre-match rain fell heavily. Some thought this might help the Woodsmen's cause, but when they trailed 2.2 to 5.1 at quarter time, any slim hope was already fading to anorexic.

That's when Murray Weideman and Hooker Harrison force-fed the Pies' skeletal flag hopes with a good 'bit of biff'.

As the Demons' stars emerged from packs clutching eyes, nose or mouth, the anger in the crowd and the Melbourne team rose. Melbourne's goals began to blur physically and metaphorically. Suddenly the Demons were more interested in the square-up than the square and when rain swept across the ground it was Melbourne who sank and Collingwood who swam.

By three-quarter time the Black and Whites were 5 goals up and they went on to win by 3 goals in one of the great Grand Final wins of all time.

For a long time there was an unshakeable belief that you had as much chance of winning a premiership from an Elimination Final as losing weight on a chocolate only diet.

Since the 1972 inception of Elimination Finals in VFL/ AFL, no one has managed it. Nobody has done it in rugby league either.

On the odd occasion when a club sneaks through into the Grand Final they get clobbered worse than a black suspect in the LAPD gymnasium.

In 1980 Collingwood, who had finished the qualifying round 5th, fronted-up against Richmond and had their score more than doubled in what was, to then, a record drubbing. The current record Grand Final deficit comes from 1988 when Melbourne made it from 5th to the Grand Final and there were hung, drawn and quartered by Hawthorn. More recently (1991) West Adelaide clawed their way from Elimination Final to Grand Final only to have their score doubled by North Adelaide. West fared a little better than Glenelg one year later. The Tigers did well from the Elimination Final to the preliminary, but that's where the joy froze. Port thrashed them 17.3 to 7.7 in the Grand Final.

No wonder then that in 1984 Norwood were given about as much chance of conquering Port as an Australian winning an Olympic fencing medal.

It wasn't just that Norwood had to come from the Elimination Final: they'd actually had to win 7 of their last 8 minor round games to make the 5.

As it happened, luck was with them. In a draw most clubs could only dream of, Norwood in their first 2 finals met Australian footy's greatest finals schmucks. South Adelaide and Centrals provided the sort of finals opposition that those clubs usually provide — none. Well, that's not entirely true, Centrals actually led by 19 points at three-quarter time but they couldn't hold off the Redlegs.

So far so good, but Glenelg were next and they were tougher

than a surf club steak. Norwood bit through.

And so they came to meet old rivals Port, who with stars like Evans, Bradley and Ebert were expected to bolt.

From the moment Craig Balme, brother of coach Neil, started to scrap with Port's Tim Evans during 'Advance Australia Fair' the game was earmarked as a war of attrition.

The Magpies led 4 times during the match, but it was Norwood, with Roberts kicking 6 goals, who triumphed by 9 points and became the first and only team ever to win a flag from an Elimination Final.

BIG DAY BIG FIZZ

The fans have waited all season. Their hopes are high. They have had their scarves and beanies dry-cleaned and kegs have been ordered and placed in waiting on the back lawn. Nervously they watch the reserves Grand Final, the excitement and fear mingling and rising in their stomach. The skydivers do their thing, then their team runs onto the ground, the coin is tossed and the ball bounced. And on the following occasions that's about where it ended for the fans whose teams were involved in the greatest non-events of footy history.

NORTH ADELAIDE V PORT ADELAIDE 1989

This may not be the biggest defeat in Grand Final history by points but there is no doubt this was the most lopsided contest since the Christians took on the lions.

North had finished on top of the ladder after the qualifying rounds, but went down to Port in the Second Semi-final by 23 points. When North came back to beat Norwood in the Preliminary most pundits thought a close game was on the cards.

That theory was blowing in the wind by half-time when Port led 9.7 to 0.3. And things got worse. At three-quarter time it was 11.11 to 1.6 and at the final, welcome, siren 15.18 to 1.8.

For North it was the ultimate in humiliation, the summit of shame, the apex of abasement. Occasionally the ball would wobble toward North's half-forward line only to be repelled by the Port defenders who seemed to have more time on their hands than a council road gang.

The game took on a mesmeric quality. Watching North was both appalling and compelling; as if some traffic accident victim was writhing on the road and you were too frozen to act. Witnessing their shameful performance almost made you feel shamed yourself.

Even some Port supporters probably found themselves tempted to view old Don Lane re-runs rather than sit through the embarrassing spectacle that passed for a Grand Final.

Mercifully it ended.

North's solitary goal was scored by Burton.

The hangover from this game lasted into the 1990 final round. In the Qualifying Final, North at half-time led Glenelg by 26 points — they wound up losing by 23. North fought back to win the First Semi-Final against South and then fronted-up to their tormentors Port in the Preliminary Final. Talk about deja-vu: at quarter time Port had kicked 10.5 to North's 1.1 and at half-time they led 17.7 to North's paltry 4.2.

As Port saved themselves for the Grand Final, North fought back to be half of Port's score at the final siren: 14.7 to 28.14.

In the last two games of 1989 and 1990 between the two clubs, Port had scored a combined 43.32 to North's 15.15

GEELONG V CARLTON 1995

Statistically the 1988 Hawthorn demolition of Melbourne (Hawthorn 22.20 defeated Melbourne 6.20) ranks as the biggest defeat in this league, but there were excuses. Melbourne had fought their way from the Elimination Final and were physically and emotionally drained by the time they got to the big day.

In 1983 an inexperienced Essendon got a steam clean by the ruthless Hawks' outfit of Alan Jeans (Hawthorn 20.20 d Essendon 8.9) in another dud game.

But these efforts were at least understandable. Not so with the Carlton-Geelong Grand Final of 1995.

Geelong had everything to play for, having the previous year been beaten for the 2nd time in 3 years by West Coast. Now they went in with the same rest as their opponents. Two easy lead-up finals had spared them the worst and yet by the first change they were suffering the sort of slaughter experienced by the diggers at Gallipoli.

The Blues' machine-gunners were Kernahan, Bradley and Spalding. They tore up the turf with Geelong blood and bone leading by 13 points at quarter time, 40 at half time, and 59 at three-quarter time and finally finishing ahead 21.15 to 11.14.

Only a spate of late goals saved Geelong the embarrassment of taking the statistical booby prize from Melbourne's 1988 team.

That it was Geelong's 4th Grand Final defeat in 7 years was the bitter icing on a very spongey effort.

SOUTH FREMANTLE V WEST PERTH 1975

What a lemon of a game. West skipped to an early lead and led by 30 points at the main break. In the third quarter they increased their margin and then in the mother-of-all last quarters, out scored South 10.5 to 1 behind. Hugh Grant put up more resistance to Divine Brown than South managed against the Cardinals.

Final scores were WP 23.17 to SF 7.9

In a personal romp, West's Barry Day kicked 7 goals in the last quarter.

The one consolation for South was that their pathetic final quarter still looks good when one compares it to that of Perth in the Subiaco-Perth First Semi-Final, 1959. Subiaco won that game 26.23 to Perth's 7.8. In the third quarter Perth were held to 1 point while Subiaco kicked 16.8!!!!

FINALS FADE-OUT

What are the worst cases of finals fade-out? Which teams snatched defeat from the jaws of the bull-terrier named victory? Who are the clubs that wasted all that money on the new flagpole and had to replace the champagne with vinegar?

There have been quite a few sudden collapses but for the most SHAMEFUL cases of FINALS FADE-OUT we nominate these:

EAST FREMANTLE V PERTH

How could you lead by 53 points at three-quarter time and still lose a final? You'd have to ask that of Perth's 1957 Preliminary Final side because they managed it. At three-quarter time Perth led by 53 points — 16.17 to 9.6. Disgruntled Old East supporters were already shuffling head-down for the train, contemplating a desolate ride back to the port while their Perth counterparts gave their kiss-curls an extra lick of Brylcream and prepared to Rock Around The Clock in celebration of winning their way into another Grand Final.

With a big rosette where his nose used to be, Easts' Norm Rogers had to be replaced at the oranges. These were the days when once you left the ground you couldn't come back. Steve

Marsh, Easts' rookie captain-coach, looked around and picked out ruckman Laurie Nugent as Rogers' replacement. If that blow on Rogers was deliberate, the hitter managed a worse strategy than John Hewson with his GST.

From the first bounce of the last quarter Nugent took control of the game. Jelly was harder to slice through than the Perth defence in that last quarter. With Easts' mosquito fleet snapping up everything Nugent sent their way East kicked an incredible 10 goals for the last quarter and won 19.10 to 17.18.

For their fabulously flimsy footy in that last quarter, the Demons of that day are inducted right at the head of FINALS FADERS.

Not that the East Fremantle team could laugh. They were already there courtesy of Perth's 1955 premiership team.

What had those Blue and Whites been doing? Staying up all night smoozing to Frank Sinatra? In the WAFL Grand Final of 1955 East Fremantle led Perth by 8.5 to 2.2 at half-time. Perth powered back in the third, but even at the next break East still led by two points with the same strong breeze at their backs that had enabled them to kick 7 goals to 0 in the second quarter.

It should have been a shoe-in, but led by triple Sandover Medallist Merv McIntosh, Perth got their nose in front and triumphed 11.11 to 11.9, casting Old Easts' 1955 Grand Finalists into the abyss of embarrassment.

EAST FREMANTLE V SWAN DISTRICTS

By 1965 ex-Melbourne ruckman Big Bob Johnson had led East Fremantle to defeats in 3 successive Grand Finals.

The previous year, 1964, pre-season rank outsiders Claremont had managed to upset the Blue and Whites in the closing moments. In 1965 The Beatles and Swan Districts had taken all before them. The Beatles were looking at a wall of gold records, Swans at a 4th flag to add to those they had won in '61, '62 and '63.

All had seemed lost for East when they finished 4th at the end of the qualifying round, but they beat West Perth in the First Semi and Perth in the Preliminary to once more face the Black and Whites — the same team that had easily defeated them in '62 and '63.

By half-time Swans had their hands on the '65 flag, leading 11.3 to 5.9. The 'premiership quarter' didn't help the port team much and at three-quarter time they were in more trouble than Larry Emdur at a talent night. With a powerful breeze at their back for the last term, Swans led 14.5 to 9.14. and their fans were breaking into renditions of The Beatles 'It Won't Be Long'.

But all those hours spent at the Melville and Broadway Stomps started to pay dividends for East. Shaking their stovepipes through a thousand Frugs and Watusis must have built up the East boys' legs. They came back. Bentley, Watson, Lewis and Martinson kicked 4 goals in 8 minutes for East to hit the front as Swans collapsed quicker than a Cairo apartment block. Swans dug in the rubble of their resolve though and emerged with a goal to snare back the lead and breathe again. Then Big Bob goaled before Swans again replied.

Finally, with Imrie, Neesham and Thornley controlling the field play, East bulldozed the last of the Swans' resistance. Watson goaled twice more and Johnson and Casserly entombed Swans in their death chamber.

Swans had the Ticket To Ride but in 1965 East owned the train.

WYNNE'S WIN

The 1978 Grand Final is one that will be remembered with great shame by all Sturt players, officials and supporters.

Up against Norwood they got off to a flying start. Maybe this was because the Norwood boys were up late listening to 'Mug's Game' and 'Never Mind The Bollocks' and were still a little sleepy.

Whatever, at half-time Sturt led by 23 points and with minutes to go in the 3rd term they had stretched the lead the way a good hangman stretches his noose. There seemed no way they could lose.

It was then that Norwood's tough man and on-field general John Wynne took a leaf out of Johnny Rotten's book. It was out with 'Take It Easy' and in with some good solid nutting and rutting. The Sex Pistols had outraged Britain with 'God Save The Queen'. Wynne didn't have Her Majesty to thumb his nose at, but he had Sturt's closest thing to royalty — coach Jack Oatey.

Waiting until the ball and a Sturt player went near the boundary line Wynne charged in, deliberately missing the player and landing in the Sturt coaching box where Ted Langridge and Bob Shearman gave 'Windows' a few how-do-you-dos. Wynne responded by ruffling Oatey's hair. This was like Paul Keating guiding the Queen with his hand — IT JUST WASN'T DONE. But Wynne DONE it anyway.

The incident so upset the Sturt brains trust that they seemed unable to cope with Norwood's last-quarter surge — Norwood adding an amazing 7.5 to Sturt's 2.5 to sneak home by a solitary point, condemning Sturt to the Hall Of Shame for the greatest fade-out in SANFL postwar history.

Valiant charger — John Wynn says hello.

Len Thompson, Max and Wayne Richardson and 'Twiggy' Dunne have the SHAMEFUL distinction of being in two of the greatest Grand Final fade-outs in recent memory.

In 1970 the great Pies' quartet were there to blow a half-time lead of 44 points against Barassi's Carlton. Seven years later against Ron Barassi's Kangaroos they scotched a three-quarter time lead of 27 points to only manage a tie. Naturally the Pies lost the replay.

What had Barass dunne? Pinched their flares while the Pies' boys dreamed of Jane Fonda, then sprinkled them in chooks' blood by the light of a full moon? Whatever he did, it was effective in '70, and the bad juju was still working 7 years down the track.

In fact it had strengthened, because the '77 fade-out was even more remarkable than its predecessor. In that '77 tied Grand Final North sucked on the oranges with only 4 goals to their name (true they'd notched a lot of points). Amazingly North almost doubled their three-quarter time score in the last quarter (North went from 4.15 to 9.22). What were those Pies doing? Yoga? Barry Cable generalled North Melbourne from a 27-point deficit at the last break to a 7-point lead. A stray Peter Moore shot brought the margin back to 6. Maybe it would have been kinder to end it there — but poor old Twiggy Dunne managed to mark and goal and tie the game, only for the Pies to be done in the replay.

But back to 1970. At half-time time Barassi did not berate his charges for their lamentable effort. He simply told them to handball and run, hoping that Collingwood would relax. They did. In a scintillating 3rd term the Blues kicked 8 goals, many by unmarked forwards. The move of Ted Hopkins onto the field as a forward was the icing on Barrassi's big cake. Hopkins kicked 3 goals for the term and 4 for the match. Still, when Len Thompson goaled in the last quarter the Pies' lead had stretched to 21 points. The Blues would not give up though.

103

Big John Nicholls drilled a couple and the colliwobbles started in earnest. After Hopkins' 4th, Crosswell kicked truly, the Blues were home.

Ron had his voodoo hoodoo working and as Deborah Conway would sing — it was only the beginning.

HAWTHORN V ESSENDON 1984

In the 1983 Grand Final Sheedy's Baby Bombers had received a Hawthorn caning right across their ingenue buttocks.

At half-time in 1984 it was looking like Yabby Jeans' was going to introduce thumbscrews on the Dons for good measure. His team led 8.6 to 3.11 and that should have been that. Even at the last break (10.8 to 5.15) the Hawks were in the box seat. But Simon Madden began to take charge of the bounce downs, and Baker and Watson, with all that raging to Cold Chisel and Australian Crawl under their belt, just ran riot.

At the final bell it was the Essendon boys that lit-up and the Hawks who copped the cheap wine.

ADELAIDE CROWS V ESSENDON 1993

Essendon were come back kings 9 years later when they went on a second-half Crow shoot. The Camry allsorts had bounded away to a seemingly unassailable half-time lead of 42 points. In fact they were exactly double Essendon at the long break: 12.12 to 6.6. But in a 2nd-half effort that had the muscular resolve of a UN resolution, the Crows pilfered a mere 2 goals from the stingy Dons. Even poor old Rocket Racer, Laurie Connell's ill-fated Perth Cup winner, had more zip in the last stanza than Adelaide, at least it made it past the post before it collapsed.

With that damn little Darren 'The Menace' Bewick kicking 6 goals and old-stager Tim Watson coming back to form, the Red and Blacks overran Adelaide 17.9 to 14.16, booking themselves a place in the GF and the Crows a permanent spot in the Hall Of Shame.

REGULAR SEASON FADE-OUT

Of course it's not just the finals where the front-runners go down like scrabble tiles in an earthquake. Here are a couple of recent blown games that covered the losers in the cloak of SHAME.

ADELAIDE CROWS V SYDNEY SWANS 1995

The 1995 Adelaide Crows followed the example of the '93 Preliminary Final team.

The '95 Crows inducted themselves into the Hall Of Shame in a Round 5 fiasco in the harbour city.

With a 3-goal break heading into the last quarter they buckled like a Demis Roussos deckchair. In that last 30 minutes the Crows kicked a solitary behind to Sydney's 11 goals 9. The word 'pathetic' doesn't adequately convey the Crows capitulation. It was so devoid of spine as to be amoebic, it was wetter than a Melbourne long weekend, it was less ballsy than a chorus of castrati, it was overwhelmingly CROWDIOUS.

The Swans finally won 20.24 to 12.15.

SYDNEY SWANS V ST KILDA 1994

Many of the same Swans that shoved Adelaide shamewards, had just a year before been bare-bummed shamed by a rapacious St Kilda.

It was night, the SCG was buzzing. Round 7 and the Swans were looking good. At three-quarter time St Kilda trailed 8.10 to 15.6.

As the Swans sucked oranges many must have already been thinking 'cointreau' or 'vodka' or 'bourbon and beefsteak'. Their fantasy had them carried shoulder-high by a phalanx of nymphettes to a giant feast where Ron Barassi cavorted, holding then-Saint Tony Lockett's head on a platter. They wanted the Plugger bad for what he had done earlier in the game to their team-mate Peter Caven.

The big Saint hit Caven full pelt with a too-high elbow and ultimately received 8 weeks. It was like putting an eggshell in the path of a locomotive. Caven's face was so badly damaged that he required corrective surgery.

That incident had seemed to inspire the Swans and as they shook off the last of their triumphant fantasy and took their positions for the last quarter they led by a whopping 38 points. But if Tony Lockett can play the Villain he is even more at home as the Hero.

In one of the greatest individual efforts ever seen, Lockett dragged the Saints back into the game, kicking 3 goals in the last few minutes (11 for the match out of 16). St Kilda hit the front in the last minute to win by a point: 16.14 to 17.7, with Big Tony's exit line a two-finger salute to the irate Swans' supporters.

A year later the same mob were cheering him as he strutted the field in their own colours.

Too late though for that '94 Swans' team — into the Hall Of Shame for that one fellas.

GEELONG V HAWTHORN 1989

The Cats have long been renowned for their attacking flair but for years there has been a question mark over their defence. As noted in other examples, many teams can compound but the Cats did their reputation no good on 7 May 1989 when they led

Hawthorn by over 50 points in the 2nd quarter, only to be beaten by 8.

Sorry Cats, we love the check-side goals, the sixty-metre torps that split the middle and the acute-angle exocets, but we still have to induct you into the Hall Of Shame for this effort.

DROPPING OUT OF THE SKY
TEAMS THAT WENT FROM PREMIERS TO LAST IN SUCCESSIVE YEARS

Only two have managed to let the champagne go completely to their heads and tumble from premiership to wooden spoon: GLENELG (1934-35) and SUBIACO (1915-16).

A little dab'll do ya. (Tony Feder/Sporting Pix.)

CHEWY ON YA BOOT

FOOTY'S MOST INEPT GOAL-KICKING
PERFORMANCES

The idea is to put the ball between the two big tall posts. Just like slotting a piece of polony between two slices of bread. But how would you like these blokes behind the lunch counter? If they made sandwiches the way they kicked, you'd find the polony in the dishwasher and the tomato sauce in the breadbin. For atrocious kicking we induct these players into the Hall Of Shame.

PLAYERS WHO HAVE KICKED THE MOST BEHINDS WITHOUT A GOAL IN A MATCH (VFL/AFL)

0.11 TOM ALLEN
RICHMOND (V NORTH MELBOURNE, 1949)

0.11 STUART SPENCER
MELBOURNE (V GEELONG, 1956)

THE MOST NUMBER OF BEHINDS TOTAL BY A PLAYER IN A MATCH (AFL/VFL)

The interesting thing about this list is that the players on it are of the highest calibre. McNamara, Coventry, Todd, Whitten and Jesaulenko are among the very greatest that ever played the game, which goes to show that to miss a lot of goals you've still got to get the ball a heck of a lot.

5.16 EDDIE JAMES
GEELONG (V ST KILDA, 1899)
1.13 DAVE McNAMARA
ST KILDA (V RICHMOND, 1922)
1.13 GORDON COVENTRY
COLLINGWOOD (V ST KILDA, 1930)
2.13 TED WHITTEN
FOOTSCRAY (V SOUTH MELBOURNE, 1956)
6.12 ALEX JESAULENKO
CARLTON (V HAWTHORN, 1969)
7.12 RON TODD
COLLINGWOOD (V RICHMOND, 1938)

Eddie James, who also kicked 1.9 in a match against Fitzroy must hereby be awarded 'chewy on ya boot' champion in perpetuity.

FINAL FLUTTERS

INACCURATE INDIVIDUALS

I wonder if ARCH THOMPSON (Geelong) tried the old trick of actually aiming for the behinds when he kicked 0.8 against Melbourne? He couldn't have done worse.

Close games are certainly going to expose any jitters and they don't come any closer than a drawn Grand Final.

Which is another way of saying that the last two guys you'd hire for the bomb disposal squad would be Arnold Briedis and Bill Brittingham.

In 1977s drawn Grand Final, North Melbourne's BRIEDIS almost matched Thompson when he kicked 0.7 in a team score of 9.22. BRITTINGHAM (1948) kicked 2.8 in football's 1st drawn Grand Final and JOHN HENDRIE of Hawthorn kicked the same score in the 1976 Grand Final.

MOST INACCURATE TEAM EFFORTS

The 1957 EAST PERTH team must have been a bunch of tremble-boots. In a game against Swan Districts they kicked 1.15 in the 2nd quarter and at one stage in the 3rd quarter were 1.26. They won the match 3.30 to 5.11

In 1923 COLLINGWOOD had 29 scoring shots — 2.27 (five posters) — and still got thrashed by Geelong, 13.14.

EAST FREMANTLE have a bad-boot radar down at the port. In 1931 they kicked 4.28 to South Fremantle's 5.8. Four years earlier they kicked 15 straight behinds but managed to finish with 9.25 against West Perth's 6.11.

In 1917 on the same day East Fremantle kicked an amazing 23.41 to Midland Junction's 4.2, South Fremantle and Perth fought out one of the all-time low scoring games, 2.10 (South) to Perth's 1.11 — talk about isolated pockets!

SOUTH FREMANTLE had miscues of their own — 1.16 v

North Fremantle in 1912 and 0.10 v East (5.15) in 1910.

RICHMOND booted a miserable 2.20 against Hawthorn in 1975.

WEST TORRENS must have had some bad juju working on their opponents. South Adelaide twice kicked 7.25 against Torrens (1937/53) and then West Adelaide kicked the identical score in 1960 against Torrens. Torrens themselves managed 6.25 against Norwood in 1941.

SOUTH ADELAIDE, never ones to be outdone when it comes to incompetence, had a horror day in 1936 when they kicked 9.32 against Glenelg. In 1922 they just bettered that with 10.32 against West.

MUG SHOTS

The 1979 SOUTH ADELAIDE PANTHERS were worse shots than those skivvied Cubans who never managed to hit Don Johnson in 'Miami Vice'.

Can you believe it: 3.14 in a Grand Final? Obviously over-awed by their first Grand Final appearance in 15 years South shot everywhere but straight on the day they went down to Port Adelaide.

Mind you, the writing was on the wall after they had 21 more scoring shots than Norwood in the First Semi-Final and only won by 21 points! (13.28 to 13.7).

Did anybody think to call Spano?

For goodness sakes, when your boys are kicking this bad, surely the master hypnotist could do something. Chopper him in or rush him from the airport with a motorcycle escort, get him to the ground and convince the lads that the space between the goalposts is the grand canyon.

In the 1988 Elimination Final STURT kicked 4.19 against Glenelg, who fared much better (15.12). Obviously nobody did call old Spano.

In the 1931 WAFL First Semi-final EAST PERTH kicked 10.19 to tie with South Fremantle 12.7. Though they won the replay their kicking didn't improve — in the 2nd game they kicked 9.18 making a combined total of 19.37 for the 2 games.

Like a lot of other things in their finals, COLLINGWOOD'S accuracy disappears up the player race.

Notable efforts include 9.28 in the 1979 Qualifying Final against North, 9.24 in the 1980 Grand Final, 9.21 in the 1934 First Semi-final and 9.20 in the 1917 Grand Final.

The worst VFL/AFL effort in modern times though is probably FITZROY'S 4.16 in the Second Semi of 1960. Maybe the Roys were just being nice, trying not to hit the elderly gentlemen in the white coats?

KING MISSES

STEPHEN OLIVER (Carlton) hit the post with his first 3 scoring shots in league football.

JOHN JAMES the Carlton Brownlow Medallist kicked 8.43 in his first season.

PETER JOHNSTON (Melbourne and Geelong 1976-86) was such a notoriously bad kick that he once feigned injury so that he wouldn't have to kick the ball. The umpire made Johnston leave the field when Gary Ablett took the kick.

Sandover Medallist STEVE MARSH kicked 32.64 in one season.

113

Swans making geese of themselves. (Tony Nolan.)

DOG DAY AFTERNOONS

WHERE THE LID FINALLY BLEW

FOOTBRAWLS

For the worst cases of footbrawl the following matches and incidents are hereby inducted into the Hall Of Shame:

EAST PERTH V SOUTH FREMANTLE 1932

The most shameful of all incidents was the death in 1932 of South Fremantle's RON DOIG as a result of injuries received in a vicious Semi-Final between East Perth and South at Leederville Oval. For some reason there had been bad blood between the teams for a long time. Back in September of 1928 after a final between the same clubs, the umpires were called before the Board to explain why no reports had been made. The press had written that match up as vicious and spiteful but the umpires claimed that players swung but did not hit, threatened but did not punch. It must have been some phantom donny-brook when you look at the free kicks: 54 to South and 48 to East Perth!

The football historian Dolph Heinrichs wrote of football in the *West* in '32, 'Football was invested with a foulness and viciousness it had not known previously and has not known since. Play was charged with venom, players were charged and flattened after kicking the leather and the uppermost idea in some of the games was to hurt rather than excel.'

SOUTH MELBOURNE V CARLTON 1945

This remains the biggest finals footbrawl of all time. The match was played at Princes Park with 62,986 fans screaming for blood. They got it in abundance. South had the week's break and an all-star cast that included Cleary, 'Basher' Williams, Matthews, Clegg and Nash. Carlton had 18-year-old Ken

'Dirty' Hands at centre half-forward and Perc Bentley coaching. By the time the game was over 6 South and 3 Carlton players had been reported. The umpires must have had writer's cramp as it took until 6.30 pm to write up their reports.

The day was cool, the ground dry — as South's skipper Matthews soon found out when Carlton's tough man Bob Chitty cleaned him up in the opening minutes. Before long Hands and Grossman were trading punches, then Carlton's Mooring upended Kelly. Things were hotting up and the umps were in strife. Then, just after Carlton had goaled to regain the lead Hands was knocked unconscious at centre half-forward and the Blues swarmed on the assumed villain, 'Basher' Williams. In turn, the Bloods jumped to Williams' aid and a vicious melee ensued which was only cleared by umpire Spokes bouncing the ball. Hands managed to recover and in the 3rd quarter goaled to sneak Carlton away. At oranges it was Carlton by 23 points. Bang! The last quarter was underway with Chitty decked behind play. Another donnybrook developed and this time police came onto the ground to restore order. They'd not long left when Carlton's winger Turner was KO'd, followed in quick succession by South's Whitfield. Now it was an all-in, and once again Spokes could do nothing but bounce the ball away from the fight and let the game recommence. Hands was again flattened after taking a mark, and then at the centre bounce Mooring was thumped after kicking the ball. Order was totally breaking down and again the police intervened. Amid the chaos, Carlton's suspended Fitzgibbon rushed onto the oval and joined the affray. He was led away, struggling, by police. After the game had resumed, Hands again took a mark and was flattened in a late charge by Cleary who was in turn 'snotted' by Carlton's Savage. Not sure if he was in a football match or under bombardment on the Kokoda Trail, Hands missed his shot for goal and during the resultant kick-in Cleary had to dodge bottles and debris. Carlton's Jim Clark recalled the game, 'Bob Chitty was an inspiration to Carlton. He decked Laurie Nash early on but Nash evened up in the last quarter — Bob copped an elbow that split his eyebrow wide open ... I was mighty glad to finish that game in one piece but there was a lot of bad feeling ... unfortunately it continued off the field.'

South's Jim Cleary was under no illusion as to the villain, Carlton's Bob Chitty: '... we ducked and weaved as best we could but Carlton seemed determined to kill us all .. football went out the window. After our tiny rover Billy Williams was knocked senseless, then Teddy Whitfield and Herbie Matthews went down, things got completely out of hand ... as the South players left the field at half-time we were pelted by bottles and rocks the size of your fist.'

Carlton won the match 15.13 to 10.15. The Carlton committee barred South from the after-match social, placing a note on the door: 'South Melbourne players and officials are not welcome in these rooms.'

The finale. South's Ted Whitfield: suspended for all games in 1946 after being found guilty of having kicked the ball away after a mark, attempting to strike a goal umpire, using abusive language to a goal umpire, and trying to conceal his number. Jack Williams: 12 weeks — 8 for adopting a fighting attitude towards the field umpire and Carlton's McClean, plus 4 for obscene and abusive language to a goal umpire. Don Grossman: 8 weeks for striking Mooring. Jack Cleary: 8 weeks for striking Hands after a mark. Herb Matthews was given a reprimand for throwing the ball away after a free kick. South's Smith was cleared of hitting Mooring. Carlton's Bob Chitty: 8 weeks for elbowing Billy Williams. R Savage: 8 weeks for striking Grossman. Ken Hands was cleared of charging into the back of Ron Clegg.

As they say, for a game of footy that was some bout!

RICHMOND V ESSENDON 1974

What a day. There were more punches than at a quintuplets' birthday party. The spark appeared to be a second quarter confrontation between Mal Brown of Richmond and Jerker

Jenkins of Essendon. As the players left the field for the break, Dons' trainer Laurie Ashley shot off his mouth at Brown. Not for long. Ashley was soon flat-out on the ground. John Cassin, Essendon's 19th man leapt onto Brown and all hell broke loose with players and officials all determined to display their pugilistic art. 'Whale' Roberts copped a broken jaw. Essendon nice guy Ron Andrews copped 6 weeks for going harpooning. Essendon fitness advisor, Jim Bradley, had a go at Brown before the Tigers' Parsons and team manager Graeme Richmond sought retribution. The result: Bradley 6 weeks, Parsons 4, Richmond (Graeme) a $2,000. fine. Brown was given just 1 week for snotting Ashley.

NORWOOD V PORT ADELAIDE 1894

The bad blood between these two clubs goes way back. Back in 1894 Norwood and Port fought out a violent game to confront South Adelaide for the flag. The *Advertiser*'s man wrote, 'It is a pity that at a time when the good name of the game is sufficiently injured by the many adverse rumours concerning the doings of the teams, that its reputation should be further sullied by disgraceful exhibitions of fighting on the field.

'Munyard of the Ports, afforded a far from edifying spectacle in front of the pavilion which was filled with ladies, by deliberately striking Carroll, of the Norwoods. Although a player came between the two, the Portonian repeated the offence and made the claret flow.'

WEST ADELAIDE V PORT ADELAIDE 1962

In 1962 the biggest postwar SA stoush erupted when Port's wingman Ken Tierney flattened West centreman Robert Day after Day had disposed of the ball. As Day's shot headed goalwards, West's captain-coach Neil Kerley headed Tierneywards. Umpire MacKay caught Kerley's late collision with Tierney and had no sooner put him in the book than a Port player rushed in and clashed with special K. This began a wild brawl. By the end of the game 4 West players had been reported: J Ryan for striking Hayes, F Hogan for striking Motely, N Kerley for charging Tierney and B Johnson for striking Tierney. Only Johnson's report related to the melee. Johnson copped 3 weeks and Kerley 2.

1910 GRAND FINAL
COLLINGWOOD V CARLTON

This must have been another stoush of epic proportions. Carlton's Percy Sheehan and Collingwood's John Shorten each were suspended for all of the following season (1911) and half of the next (1912) while Baquie (Carlton) and Baxter (Collingwood) each received 1 year.

The final round was already a bloody and violent affair prior to the Grand Final. Carlton and South had fought a bruising Second Semi-Final. After every conceivable use of elbow, knee and forearm had been employed by South Melbourne and after Carlton had lost three players in the sensational bribes scandal (*see WORST FAN BEHAVIOUR and CHEATS*), South won. In those days that didn't mean you got the break. South had to play Collingwood for the right to knock over the minor premiers, Carlton again.

When Collingwood beat South in the Preliminary they earned the right to meet Carlton in the Grand Final. One of Carlton's disqualified men was exonerated and came back for the game. Before umpire Elder had bounced the ball Carlton's Belcher had mashed the Pies' Hughes. Daykin squared-up belting Belcher. In the last quarter the Pies' rover Baxter and Carlton's Baquie fought openly. As Baquie relentlessly punched Baxter, Collingwood's Shorten threw a savage haymaker into Baquie. The boundary umpire said Baquie managed to get to his feet, king hit Hughes and then collapsed beside the prone Hughes. Police moved in on the brawl that was now an all-in with spectators climbing the fence to engage. Finally umpire Elder managed to bounce the ball and restart the game.

In an incredible twist, Collingwood claimed that it was player Daykin not Baxter who had been involved with Baquie. Daykin was not going to play again anyway and clearly didn't mind being the scapegoat. Neither the umpires, nor the press, nor the fans could believe it when Baxter was cleared at the re-hearing!

From *The Official History of the Collingwood Football Club*.

IT'S A KNOCKOUT

Behind the play incidents are not uncommon but some are stamped like the imprint of the Phantom's ring in a criminal's jaw. These incidents are hereby inducted into Footy's Hall Of Shame

WRIGHT — SOMMERVILLE

It was 1965, a Preliminary Final, Collingwood v Essendon, a packed MCG. The radio commentators were following the play in the Collingwood forward line when a growing murmur drew their attention back down the field where an Essendon player lay sprawled on the ground.

Hands on hips, standing his ground was Collingwood half-back Duncan Wright, the only other person in the vicinty. The figure on the ground wasn't moving. By the process of elimination the commentators and the 99% of people at the ground

121

(Photo: Herald-Sun.)

who did not see the incident, worked out that the prone player
was Wright's opponent, Essendon half-forward flanker John
Sommerville.

Sommerville was carted off the ground and missed the
Grand Final which Essendon won against St Kilda the

following week. Somerville came back for a couple more years at top level.

Duncan Wright, in just his 24th game for Collingwood never played league football again. He was dropped from Collingwood's 1966 list.

No charges were ever brought over the incident

REGAN — WILLIAMS

In 1967 while Jimi Hendrix was telling us all about the 'Purple Haze', East Fremantle met Subiaco at Subiaco Oval. Shortly into the 2nd quarter Subiaco scored a goal and when the dust had settled, Subiaco half-back Trevor Williams was prone, unconscious on the half-back flank experiencing a purple daze. East Fremantle utility Michael Regan was reported by a goal umpire as being the culprit, striking with a fist to the head.

Later in the game Subiaco's Peter Eakins (who later played with Collingwood) was reported for striking Regan in the inevitable square-up.

At the tribunal hearing the story that emerged was of Regan trying to speak with another East Fremantle player Harry Neesham, of Williams tagging along where he was unwanted and suffering the consequences of his eavesdropping. In spite of an attempt by East Fremantle to call public witnesses in Regan's defence, the tribunal found him guilty and suspended him for 12 months — the equivalent of a 20-week suspension as East were not threatening the finals.

By the time Regan came back, Jimi had gone from being cult hero to mainstream star with his classic rendition of Dylan's 'All Along The Watchtower'.

Peter Eakins copped 3 weeks for his efforts on Regan.

The opening siren had just gone and half the Moorabbin crowd on 8 July 1972 were just putting the sauce on the hot dog when they looked up to find Collingwood playing with 17 men. They looked again. There was something black and white on the ground: John Greening, a potential Jesaulenko had been knocked unconscious. For the next few days all the football world had its heart in its mouth. Greening did not regain consciousness for 24 hours and even then did not display his full faculties for several days.

A league investigation found that Greening's opponent, Jim O'Dea, had committed the assault and banned him for 10 weeks. O'Dea came back to play many games for the Saints. John Greening's career however was irreversibly altered. The young man who had played 94 consecutive games and could have won the Brownlow that year (he polled 14 votes in 13 completed games) never again attained the level he had reached on that day and retired in 1976 after just 107 games.

WALDRON — LATCHFORD

In 1882 Norwood and South Melbourne played a game in which a clash between Norwood's 'Topsy' Waldron and South's Latchford caused an uproar. Details of the dispute were never revealed but the scars ran deep — at least in the psychological sense. In 1885 the two clubs agreed to play again but Norwood attached two riders: Latchford was not to be selected and a communique was to be placed in the papers expressing South's regret for Latchford's behaviour in the previous clash.

NYGAARD — KERLEY

In April 1969, while Jimi Hendrix was proving himself a voodoo chile, a Norwood player was once again on the

124

receiving end of some bad juju. Damien Nygaard was knocked senseless after a clash with famed hard man Neil Kerley, at that time coaching Glenelg. Nygaard had been starring when he was felled after handballing to a team-mate. Kerley claimed in his *'Advertiser'* column '... if Damien had disposed of the ball sooner nothing would have happened ... Damien knew the chance he was taking by trying to draw me to him.'

This sounds suspiciously like 'don't try and make the K look silly boysie.' Certainly many in the crowd at the ground and many in the media thought Nygaard's broken jaw was purely and simply the result of a late and deliberate elbow.

Nygaard's Norwood team-mates thought so too. Nygaard's replacement, Barry Smith, crashed heavily into Kerley in the 3rd quarter. In the last quarter, when Kerley stationed himself on the goal line at the Parade end, bottles were thrown over the pickets. Kerley was the first player off the oval, but a girl carrying red and blue streamers kicked him and a middle-aged man struck him on the jaw.

Interestingly, a year earlier Kerley had run into some Crosstown Traffic of his own, suffering a broken jaw and losing a tooth in a game against Centrals at Glenelg.

1958 'THE AGE OF NEFARIOUS'

Something weird must have happened in the way the planets lined up in 1958. In three parts of the continent, from the South to West to East, there were some sensational and shameful punches thrown stretching the course of the season.

KNEEBONE — KRETSCHMER

The 1958 Age Of Nefarious began in Adelaide.

Port Adelaide and Norwood, as noted earlier, enjoy a fierce and physical rivalry. Anzac Day 1958 saw a few fireworks when Norwood's Kneebone was snotted behind the play by

Port's Kretschmer. Kneebone's upper lip required six stitches and was badly cut inside. Kneebone's coach, Hadyn Bunton, stood over him screaming, 'Get up, get up' but Kneebone was incapable.

The *News*' Lawrie Jervis saw to it that the incident was recorded as one of football's most notorious when he labelled it a 'King Hit'. Port hit back at the journo who was unbowed and supported by his paper. The *News* editorial titled 'SICKENING DIRT MUST STOP NOW' called the incident a 'savage physical assault against an unsuspecting player.' The article went on to catalogue other injuries that players had sustained behind the play when playing Port. It trumpeted that matches between Port and Norwood were ongoing revenge bouts, implying that something like the clan wars of the New Guinea highlands was going on in genteel Adelaide on Saturday afternoons.

Norwood decided against laying charges, but moved for independent observers to watch for such incidents.

SHEEDY — LAWRENCE
SHEEDY — ONIONS

Five months after Port and Norwood had got the Year Of The Fist underway in Adelaide, the celebration moved to Perth. The setting was the 2nd Semi-Final between East Fremantle and East Perth. Late in the game East's captain-coach, Steve Marsh, took himself off for rover Ray 'Trizzie' Lawrence. Lawrence had barely stepped into the arena when Sheedy, East Perth's captain-coach, knocked him out, right in front of the public grandstand. Sheedy, who had learned a thing or two about picking your mark when he had roomed with the great 'Basher' Williams at South Melbourne during the war, was suspended for 4 matches and missed leading his team in its premiership victory.

Though himself a former East Fremantle player, Sheedy reserved many of his best punches for his old colours. A year prior to the Lawrence knockout, East's coach, Steve Marsh, had used Sheedy's own aggression against him and won the 1957 flag. East Fremantle's 'stormy petrel' Wilson Onions had been placed on Sheedy to draw Jack into stoushes during the Grand Final. A week before the big game Sheedy had taken a trip to the change rooms of East's vanquished opponents of the Preliminary Final, Perth, and noted the sprig marks across the chest of one of their players courtesy of Onions. Jack got the idea pretty quick. As soon as Onions lined up on Sheedy, Sheedy told him, 'You put that foot near me, Wilson, you're bloody dead.' (Sheedy was one to be believed. He once wanted to swear on a bible that he was innocent of a charge laid by umpire Montgomery.) As Sheedy tells it, not long into the game Sheedy found himself on the ground and Onions' foot too close for comfort. He hit Onions with the biggest punch he could muster, shattering knuckles on Onions' reknowned cranium. Onions went to the deck, but stayed on the ground courtesy of smelling salts. Coach Marsh, a long-time friend of Sheedy had no doubt that using Onions as a stalking horse had won him the flag. Sheedy's effectiveness was curtailed. And what about Onions? He had no regrets. He says he deserved what he got from Sheedy.

'Sheedy was set to take a mark, but was pushed out of position — I called him a squib and the world caved in on me,' said Onions at the time, hastening to add there were no hard feelings. 'How could there be, Jack was my first coach.'

COLLINGWOOD V MELBOURNE

1958, The Year Of The Fist, The Age Of Nefarious, whatever else you want to call it, came to an inevitable conclusion when the Magpies single-minded aggression, some Demons supporters might say 'thuggery', overcame Melbourne's finesse. Melbourne were hot favourites to win their 4th successive flag but the Pies and first-year player 'Hooker' Harrison had other ideas. With Harrison and Weideman whacking Demon flesh every chance they got, the Pies gradually asserted physical and mental superiority. Eventually Melbourne's cohesion was broken. Their discipline went out the window, they forgot about the ball and tried to square-up. The tables turned. With the Melbourne stars' faces looking like choice hamburger mince, Collingwood held the trophy aloft. One crazy footy season was over.

AND A HOST OF OTHERS

KICK A MAN WHEN HE'S DOWN

North Melbourne's FRED RUTLEY (1925) was suspended for life on a kicking charge after a vicious game at Geelong. He returned to the field in 1930 after the suspension was lifted.

Hawthorn and Victorian full-forward JOHN PECK was involved in a sensational incident when he KO'd South Australia's Sawley in a 1963 State game. In his 1963 defence Peck claimed Sawley had kicked him. Witnesses told the tribunal that ever since childhood Peck had a phobia of being kicked.

OLD LOYALTIES DIE QUICK

Playing for Melbourne, former South Melbourne man LEN INCIGNERI flattened South's Payne in a 1915 game causing an all-in. Play was held up for 15 minutes when the crowd invaded the oval. Incigneri copped an 8-week suspension.

IN THE BLOOD

Jack Sheedy's uncle (*see JACK SHEEDY in this section*) JUDDA BEE was a legend in Western Australian football. He was the first man to coach three clubs. He was also a specialist at removing a swag of opposition players by himself. Subiaco were highly fancied to win one Grand Final against Bee's East Fremantle, until Bee knocked out Penberthy and Diggins, two of their stars. East went on to win that one. Bee was a multiple-assault specialist.

In a 1930 derby the charge sheet read: G Bee (East Fremantle) charged with attempting to strike Shannahan, for striking Loveridge, for striking Robertson in the face with the ball and striking E. Lawn. Bee got 6 weeks.

LONG MEMORY

Norwood and St Kilda played a pre-season scratch match back in 1970. The Saints proudly displayed their new recruit, JOHN McINTOSH, and Norwood theirs, JOHN WYNNE. Wynne pretty smartly cracked McIntosh and was paid the obligatory visit by Saints' big Carl Ditterich who stood over Wynne while he was on the ground, announcing how he would gain retribution. Wynne managed to power his shoulder into Carl's knee, which took him down. Then St Kilda's STUART TROTT got involved and got belted in the nose.

Some 25 years later, the still nose-troubled Trott was in Western Australia watching a game when a young kid with a black eye came up to the crowd with whom Trott was standing.

When the boy left Trott asked what had happened to him and was told the boy had been hit in the eye by a stray can thrown at a footy match.

'You might know the kid's father,' said somebody. 'John Wynne.'

'Bloody John Wynne. That mongrel's given me a lifetime of nose surgery,' steamed Trott, 'bring the kid back here and I'll punch his other eye.'

THE WORST CASES OF
UMPIRE ABUSE BY PLAYERS

Sometimes it's physical, sometimes it's verbal, but as long as the game is played there will be times when players assault the umpire.

R P J CONDON V UMPIRE CRAPP

On 16 September 1900, Collingwood's RICHARD CONDON, the highest-profile player in the game, was disqualified for life by the VFL for using bad language to the unfortunately named Umpire Crapp. What did he say? 'That's a load of (mumbled sounds as he bites his tongue) ... Crapp!' Apparently, among the abuse Condon hurled was, 'Your girl's a bloody whore.' It was the culmination of a bad season for the Pies' captain who had received 3 weeks suspension for umpire abuse on one occasion, fought with his own ruckman (Robson) on another and tried to get his team to leave the field against Geelong in protest at the umpiring of Gibson.

After the Crapp fiasco, the Collingwood committee decided to expel Condon from the club, but withdrew this decision once the VFL delegates gave their captain a life sentence. Two years after the uproar, Collingwood once more supported Condon to return to the league, which he did in 1902.

PHIL CARMAN V GRAHAM CARBERY

A run-of-the-mill day for Essendon's Phil Carman. He'd just whacked big Gary Sidebottom (did Sidey ever win a blue in his life?) when boundary ump Carbery started to encroach on Carman's personal space. Carman simply 'nutted' him.

130

Carbery staggered backwards, reaching for report implements even as he reeled.

In his report, Carbery said that he had told Carman he was being reported and Carman had pushed him away. When he had come back at him, Carman had head butted him. Carman got 4 weeks for Sidebottom and 16 for Carbery.

BRETT AND DEAN FARMER
V UMPIRE HEARNE

It's difficult to know what to make of the events surrounding the reserves match between Perth and West Perth on 7 July 1986.

That what began as a minor infraction should somehow escalate into a whirlwind that sunk the careers of two players leaves the observer feeling that the whole thing was a needless tragedy.

Rarely, if ever, has there been a more Dog Day Afternoon, that's for sure.

The fiasco began when a couple of decisions went against Perth, and Perth's Brett Farmer was reported for time-wasting by umpire Hearne. This really sent the cyclone on its way.

With cool heads in charge the event could have ended there. Many coaches may have sensed what was about to happen and pulled a player from the ground before he got himself into deeper water. But with Mal Brown calling the shots for Perth, it was like pouring petrol on a bushfire.

In Hearne's evidence at the tribunal he noted that Brett Farmer began to abuse and threaten him after being told he was on report for time-wasting. So Hearne reported Farmer for that too. Brett's brother, Dean, appeared on the scene abusing Hearne also, and then bumping the umpire over. According to tribunal evidence he also abused umpire Tonti. Another Perth player, Glen Ugle, was also reported for interfering with Hearne.

By now there was the potential for real damage to be done

and Mal Brown decided to pull Perth from the ground. When he entered the arena he had an altercation with West Perth and ex-Fitzroy player Peter Murnane.

It was not the first time that Brown had been in trouble for ordering his team from the ground. He had done that in a pre-season game when coach of South Fremantle in 1981.

The tribunal was in for a busy night. Mal Brown was fined $5,000 personally, with a $4,000 fine for Perth for pulling the team from the ground. Brett Farmer was charged with time-wasting and abuse, found guilty on both charges and given 4 weeks concurrent. Dean Farmer was charged with abusing Hearne, abusing Tonti, and manhandling Hearne. He was found guilty on all three charges and suspended for the balance of the season and all of the next.

But like a Hollywood thriller, the drama was not yet ended.

After the hearing there was a commotion in which umpires Hearne and Tonti claimed they were further threatened and Hearne was pushed down the stairs.

Recalled to give evidence, Hearne said that Brett Farmer had told him, 'I don't care if I get four weeks, four months or four years, but I will get you,' and had then pushed him in the head and shoulder. This offence netted Farmer a 10-year ban — virtually a career. In March 1987 the bans on the Farmers were reduced, but by then the damage was done and the players' careers over.

E J BENNETTS V UMPIRE CURRIE

In the 1929 Semi-Final between West Adelaide and Norwood, there was a sensation when West's Bennetts was reported by umpire Currie for 'hacking' at him. On the ground from a bump, Bennetts reportedly 'hacked the umpire' as the umpire tried to leap over him. The charge was found proved and Bennetts was suspended for the rest of the final round and for the next 3 years. Bennetts served his sentence and later returned to again play for West, guaranteed of a place in Footy's Hall Of Shame.

Surely the most amazing player-umpire conflagration was that between MURRAY WEIDEMAN (then player-coach of West Adelaide) and umpire Bob Hall.

In 1968, immediately after a fiery North Adelaide–West Adelaide clash, Weideman told his chairman he had been abused by Hall. On Channel 7's 'World of Sport', Weideman said that after he had queried why Hall had made a decision the umpire had replied, 'You play the ball you'll find out.' When Weideman retorted he was playing the ball, he alleged the umpire swore at him. While West and their coach considered whether or not to go ahead with charging the umpire, Glenelg coach Neil Kerley urged caution on Weideman, saying umpires never forget. Kerley was proved perspicacious when the very next week, Weideman was reported for striking South's Alan Teasdale, a charge on which Weideman was exonerated.

West had in the meantime gone ahead with charging umpire Hall in relation to the previous match, but this hearing had to be postponed until the Weideman-Teasdale hearing had been completed.

On Tuesday 23 July the charge laid by West against Hall was heard. Hall did not dispute using some of the language credited to him by Weideman but claimed that it was not directed at the player in particular, but at the player's claim that he had been going for the ball.

The tribunal found the charge unsustained on the basis that the language was not abusive unless directed at a person.

THE WORST FAN BEHAVIOUR

Any fan will tell you that one of the best things about going to the footy is abusing players and umpires. Shouting at your TV set doesn't quite give you the same satisfaction as harpooning a player or ump with a well-aimed barb. Sometimes though, fans go too far. The selection below is just a tiny sample of some of the more spectacular SHAMEFUL fan behaviour.

KILL THE UMP

Fans have never been particularly fond of umpires. On any given match day around 50% will hate the ump because their team lost. Even so, the reaction these days is like a Disney movie compared to what happened at the turn of the century when an umpire incurred the displeasure of the crowd.

NORTH MELBOURNE V COLLINGWOOD 1896

In 1896 when Collingwood beat North Melbourne in a close match, the *Argus* reported that the moment the bell rang a multitude rushed to attack Roberts, the umpire. Players formed some sort of protection and 'It was well they did so, or Roberts would have been killed or seriously injured, for the moment he stepped through the gate scores of men rushed him like wolves and a scene of incredible tumult followed. Fists and sticks were going and one man in the thick of the crowd with some implement wrapped in paper was making desperate efforts to fracture someone's skull.'

As Roberts was grabbed by the hair by the mob, Collingwood's Proudfoot — a sixteen-stone policeman — snatched him free and carried the umpire through the crowd. Proudfoot had to hold one arm over his head to shield himself from the blows and received such a bad beating that one of the perpetrators was given a three-month jail term. Many Collingwood players had to fight their way to safety and North's McDougall was knocked unconscious.

According to the *Argus* a shrill voiced 'lady' had started the fracas, striking Roberts on the face at half-time. Apparently such behaviour was not all that uncommon. The *Argus* claimed that some women would spit in the players faces or wreak havoc with their long hatpins.

From *The Official Centenary History of the Collingwood Football Club.*

FREMANTLE V ROVERS 1892

Four years earlier, on the other side of the country in Fremantle, an umpire Croft was at the centre of a substantial riot.

Again, it was a case of the home side, Fremantle, losing. That they lost to Rovers, the side with whom umpire Croft had played just two years previously inflamed the situation. The fact that Croft had been reprimanded for fighting in his last game perhaps convinced the crowd that he was not to be trusted.

A report of the game states but for the presence of Constable Bonner on mounted duty at the ground, serious injuries would have occurred. At first a crowd gathered outside the pavilion hooting the Rovers players.

When the umpire appeared there was 'a general rush' at him with somebody throwing a bucket of water over him. Then the umpire was thrown against the wall. 'Matters were beginning to look serious when Constable Bonner charged the mob, but his efforts were at first unsuccessful.' Fremantle players rushed to the umpire's aid and 'The umpire got away from the wall while mounted troops kept the crowds back.'

When the umpire left the ground under escort, the jeering crowd followed down Adelaide and High Streets to the train station.

DOES YOUR CHEWING GUM LOSE ITS FLAVOUR?

It's not just the men in white who can cop problems from the crowd though, as JACK MORIARTY (Essendon and Fitzroy, 1922-33) found out in a game at Carlton.

Moriarty was stricken after accepting some chewing gum that had been laced with poison.

WALK A MILE IN MY SHOES

God those Carlton supporters are devious: on the morning of the 1915 Grand Final, Collingwood's MALCOLM 'DOC' SEDDON (at that stage enlisted in the army) was sent on a 10-mile march.

The march was ordered by a supporter of Carlton, Collingwood's rivals that day for the flag!

BLOOD FOR THE BLOODS

Another Carlton triumph in crowd intimidation came during the 1945 Grand Final against South Melbourne (*see DOG DAY AFTERNOONS — FOOTBRAWLS*). Played at Princes Park, the Blues obviously had a home-crowd advantage and when South went to their rooms at half-time they were pelted with bottles and rocks.

THE LIONS' DEN

Fitzroy supporters might have everybody's sympathy these days, but just after the Great War it was a different story. Those Roy fans did not like losing, as evidenced by the two following tales.

IVOR WARNE-SMITH (Melbourne, 1919 and 1925-32)

was doing such a good job on Fitzroy's star Merrick that the Roy supporters pelted him with stones.

TED OHLSON (Richmond, 1908-15) received a letter threatening him with injury if he played in a match against Fitzroy. Ohlson exposed the threat and played so the intimidation did not achieve its goal. One can only wonder though, how often the ploy worked!

HOLDEN LION HITS AND RUNS

GEORGE HOLDEN (Fitzroy, 1908-19) was no shrinking violet and in 1911 he had a personal war going with Essendon. He was reported by Essendon for striking their player Ogden. Earlier in the year Essendon's Martin had faced civil charges for hitting Holden.

But it was not a Dons supporter foolish enough to tangle with Holden at the end of a 1914 game. That honour went of course to a Saints' fan. Holden despatched his assailant with a G.M.H (God allMighty Hit) that had the Saints' fan up above the clouds until the smelling salts brought him back down.

CATCH ME IF YOU CAN

During a scratch match at Lathlain Park in the 1970s, an East Fremantle supporter was giving hell to Perth's brilliant but volatile half-forward MURRAY COUPER. A constant stream of invective flowed from the dimunitive fellow whose voice had the irritating screech of a yapping terrier. Throughout the game the fan abused both Couper's physical appearance (Couper had facial reconstruction) and his playing ability. When the siren rang, Couper ran towards his tormentor and leapt the fence. The yapper was a bit of a hare and he had no wish to have a one-on-one discourse with the Demon. He split for the exit with Couper in pursuit as the crowd gaped. The terrier was snared at the gate by two Perth supporters, but fortunately Couper kept his retribution to threats and chest poking.

Late in his career Couper found himself playing for East Fremantle where, as onlookers held their breath, the forward and the terrier finally buried the hatchet.

The terrier had it lucky compared to some other fans who gave the target of their abuse a chance to retaliate. Perth's NUGGET HILTZ leaned over the fence and smacked a tormentor in the kisser; East Fremantle's LAURIE NUGENT did the same; Subiaco butcher, Fred Welsh, in one feisty moment took on JOHN DUCKWORTH; and East's legendary supporter, Alby Hunter, jumped the fence to shape up to Swan District's JOE LAWSON — a policeman at that!

East Fremantle and West Perth had many a tough encounter at Leederville Oval that resulted in player and spectator confrontation. In 1980, in the match that saw West and Norwood player BRIAN ADAMSON have his jaw shattered, East Fremantle and Hawthorn player and coach, KEN JUDGE (who was not the cause of Adamson's injury), was spat upon and assaulted as he walked to the change room through a hostile members' area. Judge gave better than he got.

The game was very close and when East Fremantle won the crowd erupted.

In scenes reminiscent of the sacking of the US Embassy in Iran, police were stretched to prevent serious injury to umpires, players and spectators.

After several arrests order was restored. Charges were laid and offenders convicted in the courts.

Any supporter with any sense stayed well clear of MAL BROWN. On one occasion Mal cleaned up several hoons who were standing behind his coaching box baiting him. On a different occasion at Fremantle Oval, somebody obviously decided that if you were to confront Big Mal it better be at long distance and so hurled a billiard ball at Brown, then coaching South Fremantle, from his own members' area.

This game could have easily found its way into FADE-OUTS or DOG DAY AFTERNOONS.

Just before half-time West led by a comfortable 25 points. Then West captain, Faehse, knocked over Port's Boyd, causing an all-in. When the siren went and the West players tried to get to their dressing-room under the Sir Edwin Smith stand at Adelaide Oval, via the Members stand, they were attacked by angry Port supporters. Trainer John McCracken had two teeth knocked out and the players were shoved and heckled.

The whole incident unsettled West, and Port came back to win the game. Wests' Wright could have won the match in the dying moments but hit the post to tinge a sour day with even more vinegar.

BABE

Animal rights activists weren't very happy when some Sydney fans let a piglet loose onto the SCG in a 1993 match between the Swans and St Kilda. The piglet was marked with the word 'Plugga' in obvious homage to the Saint full-forward, TONY LOCKETT, who was out injured that day. Or was he? Maybe Tony had crossed swords with Samantha and Endora and they'd made his bacon for the day? The piglet held up play for some minutes as both officials and players made themselves look like a bunch of pork chops in trying to catch the little squealer. Finally it was left to Swan Darren Holmes to apply the perfect tackle.

A BONSER BLOKE

We conclude with a light-hearted tale of fan support. A Subiaco supporter, LES BONSER, became the best-known outer voice in Western Australia footy from the mid-70s until the entry of the West Coast Eagles.

Among Bonser's achievements were making boundary umpire WALKINSHAW a household name ('controversial boundary umpiring Walkinshaw') and cajoling a drop-kick from Stan Magro in the last year of Stan's career.

One of Bonser's favourite barracking techniques was to elongate his calls. Thus, Mark Zanotti became Zambotti and then Zamthepaymasterbotti. When Zanotti explained in the media that he had quit his job as a paymaster after he felt its boredom affected his game, Bonser's call became 'Go Zamusedtobeapaymasterbutlastyearihadalotofboredombotti'.

Sadly the entry of the Eagles devalued the WAFL comp to such an extent that Bonser could no longer attack his barracking with gusto. The Eagles games themselves, with their General-Public-Lowest-Common-Denominator conformity were not the right forum for Les either, and so one of the great voices of the game was lost in the wash of Yankese sportsspeak that today passes as commentary.

SUSTAINED MALEVOLANCE

PLAYERS WHOSE CAREER WAS A HOMAGE TO HOSTILITY

THE BELLIGERENT 7

Some players don't carry a chip on their shoulder, they have a whole forest perched there. They made their careers a homage to intimidation, pieces of performance art that celebrated the backhand, the straight right and the bent elbow.

These Belligerent 7 are such players.

DON 'MOPSY' FRASER

In *Wildmen Of Football*, his great study of football hard men, the mighty JACK DYER allowed Mopsy to tell his own terrifying story.

Beginning as a skinny kid with Richmond, 'Mopsy' grew into a behemoth — at least in the eyes of opposition players and supporters. A photo in Dyer's book makes Mopsy look like a cross between the Yeti and King Kong. The thighs are like sides of buffalo, the arms long and muscular with giant dumbell knuckles almost dragging on the ground. One is tempted to believe that this player, whom Dyer felt was the most hated in the game, was created by Dyer through some devious alchemy deep in the bowels of Punt Road. No doubt about it, Mopsy's record is every bit as terrifying as Frankenstein's Monster.

Ken Piesse* notes that Fraser copped at least 51 confirmed weeks of suspension and possibly as many as 84. The man, said by Dyer to be the 'most rugged and vicious I encountered', played 124 games at Richmond over 8 years (1945-52) being booked 6 times for 16 weeks suspension. He captain-coached Port Melbourne and East Launceston, his rogue elephant displays undiminished.

Initially Dyer told Fraser that he thought he was a 'bit frightened'. Fraser bulked up with some timber cutting and when shifted to the back line, he found his home. Nobody would ever again tell Fraser he was a 'bit frightened' and remain standing.

Steve Marsh, the great Western Australian rover, an ant compared to Mopsy, was scared of nobody on the footy field but he admits to finding Mopsy intimidating. Marsh recalled his first meeting with Fraser, 'I kicked the ball and stopped to watch it travel upfield. Whack. I was on the deck with a numb face and Mopsy standing over me. Fortunately big Merv McIntosh pushed him away and said, "Pick on somebody my size." '

Collingwood's Twomey brothers were others to feel the Fraser fury. Mopsy would pick his mark and 'bang' — one less standing.

In *Wild Men Of Football* Mopsy recounts a Victoria Park match in which he cleaned up all three brothers during the match and then a soldier foolhardy enough to run at him as he left the ground. The Pies' supporters besieged the dressing-room until a police escort got Mopsy and Jack Dyer out.

In Ted Whitten's first league game at Punt Road in 1951, Mr Football learned all about what it meant to play with the big boys. Playing on Mopsy, Ted scored a goal with his first kick. 'That's the biggest mistake you ever made, son. You won't see the game out,' said Mopsy. Late in the third quarter, as Whitten ran the same way as the ball he heard Mopsy say, 'This is it kid.' It was. Whitten was carted off on a stretcher.

Whitten claimed Mopsy had ankle tapped him at the start of the game and Mopsy was happy to admit it. Fraser's explanation says a lot about his approach to the game.

'He was there, in a man's game. You don't give a raw kid any more latitude than you would give an experienced campaigner.'

For sustained malevolence, Don 'Mopsy' Fraser is inducted as one of the Belligerent 7.

* From *The Complete Guide to Australian Football.*

Robert Muir greets Keith Grieg. (Herald-Sun.)

Unlike Mopsy Fraser, Robert Muir played in an era when a player's on-field actions could be captured in the reality of videotape and transmitted in slow motion to lounge rooms across the nation. Where the deeds of the pre-1950s players could only be told through print or hearsay, the deeds of today's players are matters of record ... most of the time. There are still incidents the cameras don't capture, leagues where video has not poked its unwanted nose into the on-field melee. But such video-free zones are the exception not the rule nowadays.

When the public clamped eyes on Robert 'Mad Dog' Muir they almost couldn't believe that he was real, but they knew that tape didn't lie.

Robert Muir was reported in almost every year of his career (1976-93). He was reported in different leagues in different States for different offences. Both players and officials felt the wrath of Robert 'Mad Dog' Muir. Muir and mayhem went hand in hand.

The first time Muir came to the public's notice was 1976, on report for striking Brownlow Medallist Peter Moore. Moore denied being punched though he did recall hard contact. Muir got off. He wasn't so lucky a year later. One week after being exonerated of tripping an umpire in a reserve's match, Muir copped 8 weeks for kicking Footscray's Smedts in another reserves game. Umpire Cameron had no doubt what had happened — Smedts had slipped over and Muir had made a vicious deliberate kick into the prone player. The following year Muir was outed for a month for striking dual Brownlow Medallist Keith Greig. The Moorabbin match was only 4 minutes old when Greig was being helped to his feet by trainers, blood streaming from his nose as boundary ump McQueen wrote Muir's name in the book. In his evidence McQueen noted a round-arm from Muir, who was pursuing Greig, had caused the injury. Muir said Greig threw his arms up and fell over. 'There was no punch whatsoever. If I had punched him he probably wouldn't have got up,' said Muir in his defence.

Muir was a terrifying spectacle when he had downed an opponent. Some players clear off and try to lose themselves in the blur of play. Not Robert Muir. He would stand over their prone body like a conquering warrior as if willing them to stand so he could smite them again.

Four weeks after resuming from the Greig suspension, Muir got another 8 weeks for kicking. South's Michael Wright removed his shirt at the Tribunal to reveal a stopmark above his ribcage.

When Muir came back against Carlton, Blues wingman Dennis Collins had a couple of smart comments to make. A right forearm to the head and down went Collins. The cameras rolled as Muir ran from the ground, managing to catch the foolish Saints' kid who went up for a congratulatory backslap and wound up the recipient of a Muir backhand.

Muir moved to South Australia the way Germany's panzers moved to Czechoslovakia. Once more he was up for such run-of-the-mill fare as kicking opponents, striking trainers and shoving umpires.

Then back to St Kilda went Muir, the cameras catching him flattening the taunting Pies' captain, Ray Shaw. Muir claimed he had only punched Shaw for spitting on him.

These incidents were only low-level rumbles on the Muir seismograph. His Vesuvius came in a match against Carlton in 1984 when he was reported, a VFL record, 7 times. Charges were: striking Val Perovic with a forearm, disputing a decision, and a report, using threatening behaviour towards umpire Kevin Smith, head-butting Bruce Doull, use of bad and abusive language to a goal umpire and striking Alan Montgomery with a fist. Not even the Raging Bull, Jake La Motta could have stopped Muir that day.

Carlton coach David Parkin stirred the pot when he claimed that it was a day that the order-off rule might have been useful.

Muir was in fact sin-binned in the Western Plains competition in 1993. Shortly afterwards the goal umpire, the president of Muir's opposing club, was being dragged over the fence. Muir received 2 years less 5 games.

For a fullsome rundown on Robert Muir's qualifications to be one of the Belligerent 7 read Jack Dyer and Brian Hansen's *Wild Men of Football, Vol. 1.*

RODNEY GRINTER

A half-back with strength and speed, Rod Grinter (Melbourne 1985-94) had an AFL career whose every panel was scraped by reports and dented by suspension.

A Grinter speciality was to arrive late on the scene with a raised forearm or elbow.

The targets wound up bruised if they were lucky, wired together if they were not. Grinter played it hard and suffered the consequences.

Reported 10 times with 31 weeks of suspensions, Grinter's most notorious effort was the 1988 felling of Footscray's Terry Wallace.

Wallace wound up with a jaw in more pieces than the former Soviet Union.

The incident went unreported but an inquiry found Grinter guilty and handed out a 6-week suspension.

MICHAEL REGAN

Not a big man — just five foot ten inches with a wiry frame, East Fremantle's Mike Regan was a clever utility, best suited to half-forward and ruck-roving. From his early days in the reserves in 1959 Mike was in trouble with the umpires and the league itself. Two striking charges were both sustained bringing him 3 weeks' suspension. Then he was found guilty of playing under an assumed name in another league: 3 weeks. Striking charges brought Regan 4-week penalties in 1962 (seconds) and 1963. Regan was quick and deadly with his fists: a knockout specialist as West Perth's Robert Hebbard found out in a game at Leederville Oval. Just as East Fremantle boasted three Regan brothers, so West Perth sported three Hebbard brothers. Colin Hebbard was the smiling assassin who once took on East Perth, knocking out legendary tough guy Mal Atwell, and inflicting damage on Dobbie Graham and Graeme John. On this occasion though it was Robert Hebbard who incurred Michael Regan's displeasure — almost with disastrous consequences.

Trevor Sprigg (another legendary enforcer) was playing fullback for East Fremantle when he saw Hebbard in the hands of trainers being carried around the boundary line behind him. Sprigg recalls seeing Hebbard turning blue and making a comment to the effect that the player was in trouble. The West Perth player had swallowed his mouthguard. Fortunately the trainers got it out.

Not long after the Leederville Oval incident, East Fremantle and West Perth were due to meet in a final round game at Subiaco.

Toby Regan, patriarch of the Regan clan, stated in the press that Mike was in fear of his life.

The match though passed without incident.

It is rumoured that many years later, a square-up did take place off the field.

It was not to be the Hebbard incident, however, that etched Mike's name in the WAFL record books. That honour went to the Trevor Williams knockout of 1967 (*see DOG DAY AFTERNOONS*). Found guilty, Mike was suspended for 12 months: a penalty that translated to 20 weeks.

In all Michael Regan racked up 34 weeks of penalties to put him at the top of the WAFL bad-boy pile until Mal Brown was able to replace him there.

After his league career finished Michael captain-coached in amateur football for a number of years. In trademark bare feet, Michael would roam the ground like a wolf hunting sheep. The sickening slap of flesh hitting flesh would echo round the ground, a player would be seen holding his head or flat-out on the ground, but there was never a boot print in the grass to identify the attacker.

South Melbourne ruckman Boyd played 60 games (1957-61) and missed 30 through suspension. At the tribunal he had a perfect record — 7 appearances for 7 convictions. Two of his appearances related to Carlton's John Nicholls.

In 1961 Boyd was sent down for 8 weeks for striking Nicholls and rover John Heathcote.

The skin on Boyd's knuckles had barely grown back when South and Carlton clashed at Princes Park. Boyd once again tangled with Nicholls but the affray went unreported.

That night on television Nicholls gave his account and, as one might expect, exonerated himself from any misdemeanour against Boyd. Boyd was not to be out-mediaed though. In a newspaper article he claimed that Nicholls had threatened him during the game and he had warned Nic, 'If you do that, I'll knock your head off.' He then claimed at a boundary throw-in Nicholls had driven his boots into his groin. Boyd had up and hit the Blues man with everything he had.

This was not a wise course of action. Hauled before the tribunal and given 12 weeks, Boyd promptly retired.

Nicholls denied the kicking allegations.

RON ANDREWS

Every street-fighter ploy in the book was in Ron Andrews' match-day manual. The raised elbow, the eye gouge, the back-hander, the straightaway right are all implements that make the Essendon-Collingwood and West Adelaide player a natural for the Belligerent 7. Big or small, bald or blond, 'Rotten' Ron was unfazed in taking them on. One moment John Cassin was his Essendon ally as Andrews king-hit 'Whale' Roberts, broke his jaw and copped 6 weeks for the trouble. The next moment Cassin was in a different guernsey being snotted by his old team-mate. Andrews' fighting was a bit like his footy, no finesse but plenty of stamina. The players on the receiving end of Andrews' aggro were numerous: Phil Maylin (5 weeks), Bernie Quinlan (2), Grame Bond (4), DiPierdomenico (4) were some officially recognised. Stewart Gull and Mark 'Jacko' Jackson were two who managed to return the hospitality in kind. Collingwood's Des Herbert almost died when Andrews body-sapper burst a hernia and one umpire was knocked unconscious by Andrews in Ballarat. No doubt about it, Andrews deserves to be part of the 7.

MAL BROWN

Mal Brown (Richmond, East Perth, South Fremantle) is easily the most-reported person to have been involved in Western Australian footy, but Mal has been charged so often and in so many different situations and been given so many varied penalties that it is virtually impossible to properly quantify charges and penalties. Many of the penalties meted out were for a calendar time and involved pre-season penalties. On at least two occasions the WA tribunal was asked to hand out penalties to Brown for incidents that occurred interstate and these also confuse the issue.

Most of Brown's offences involve clashes with officialdom. In his WAFL career the player related charges included: striking John Wynn, Bill Dempsey, Leon O'Dwyer, Bob Shields and Bob Page plus attempted kicking of Tony Morley. For these charges, all sustained, he received a total of 13 weeks suspension. He was suspended for all 1973 scratch matches for the infamous Carlton Clobbering in the 1972 post-season Carlton v East Perth match, in which Brown took out at least 4 Carlton players.

One example of Brown's affability was his treatment of a then rookie Tony Buhagiar. 'Budgie', a teenager the size of one of Mal's boot stops was minding his own business when Mal ran past and docked him with an elbow. The innocent Buhagiar assumed a case of mistaken identity. 'What'dya do that for?' He asked nonplussed in the manner of many a player before and after him. Brown crooked a finger for Buhagiar to come closer but the rookie was catching on — he moved towards Big Bad Mal but kept out of reach. Mal crooked the finger again, a cautious Budgie leaned in — which was when Mal let fly with a spitball in the face.

In his capacity as coach, Brown faced numerous charges over half-a-dozen incidents. Many of the charges were dismissed, on some occasions he was fined or cautioned and in the most severe penalty was disqualified as an official for 12 months. In his total career of WAFL and VFL football, Brown received approximately 50 weeks of suspensions as a player and 14 months in suspensions as a coach.

THE MOST-REPORTED PLAYERS

What a team you can construct from the most reported players of the game. Not that they'd ever have to take the field — chances are their opponents would rather forfeit.

The statistic 'LOST/GAMES PLAYED' shows the percentage arrived at when a player's games lost to suspension are divided by the games he actually played. Rod Grinter for example, was suspended for a total of matches that equalled nearly a quarter of the games he actually played.

Robert Muir and Phil Carman's stats do not include games played or penalties in the SANFL.

BACKS	MARK LEE	RON ANDREWS	DON SCOTT
NUMBER OF CHARGES	13	9	11
MATCHES SUSPENDED	19	24	11
LOST/PLAYED GAMES	8%	15%	4%

HALF-BACKS	ROBERT MUIR	ROGER MERRETT	ROD GRINTER
NUMBER OF CHARGES	18	11	10
MATCHES SUSPENDED	41	13	31
LOST/PLAYED GAMES	60%	4%	23%

CENTRES	DAVID RHYS-JONES	GREG WILLIAMS	GARY ABLETT
NUMBER OF CHARGES	25	15	12
MATCHES SUSPENDED	22	21	15
LOST/PLAYED GAMES	12%	10%	6%

HALF-FORWARDS	MICHAEL CONLAN	DERMOTT BRERETON	PHIL CARMAN
NUMBER OF CHARGES	14	17	9
MATCHES SUSPENDED	14	39	24
LOST/PLAYED GAMES	7%	18%	24%

FORWARDS	DALE WEIGHTMAN	TONY LOCKETT	MARK JACKSON
NUMBER OF CHARGES	15	10	13
MATCHES SUSPENDED	19	21	11
LOST/PLAYED GAMES	7%	10%	13%

FOLLOWERS	CARL DITTERICH	GREG WILLIAMS	JIM KRAKOUER
NUMBER OF CHARGES	19	16	22
MATCHES SUSPENDED	30	21	31
LOST/PLAYED GAMES	10%	10%	13%

INTERCHANGE	GREG BURNS	KARL LANGDON	ROBERT DIPIER-DOMENICO
NUMBER OF CHARGES	11	9	9
MATCHES SUSPENDED	14	13	18
LOST/PLAYED GAMES	8%	13%	7%

RESERVE	MICHAEL REGAN
NUMBER OF CHARGES	7
MATCHES SUSPENDED	38
LOST/PLAYED GAMES	30%

153

Mal could make the team as a player (games 203; matches suspended 46; lost/played games 23%), but there is no question he should be coaching the SHAMERS. Brown's decision to send Claremont player John Colreavy back onto the ground after he had been replaced and contrary to the existing rules, may have been visionary but it was yet another act which suggested the egocentric Brown believed he was bigger than the game. Twice Brown pulled a team from the field. Once at South Fremantle he probably had good cause. The game was only a scratch match and Brown believed an opposition player was out there purely to head-hunt. When one of his players came off with a broken jaw, Brown had had enough.

When Brown was banned as a coach from entering the field and therefore could not address his players on the oval at the quarter breaks, he had a large tent erected that extended over both sides of the pickets. This enabled him to talk to his players in private without them leaving the ground and without him entering it. On another occasion he had a cherry-picker carry him over the fence, but not actually onto the surface of the oval.

No doubt about it, for his contempt of authority and unparalleled sustained hostility to umpires and opponents, Mal Brown is inducted into the Hall Of Shame as coach of the Shamers.

ONE-MAN WAR
WILSON ONIONS — WA'S SECOND MOST-REPORTED PLAYER

Between 1955 and 1960, East Fremantle's WILSON ONIONS conducted a one-man war against West Perth. Onions copped 2 weeks for kicking West's Marinko in a reserves game in 1955, had a striking charge against West's Schofield dismissed in 1957, received 3 weeks for charging West's Laurie McNamara in May of 1960 in a reserves match and then a further 3 weeks for charging Richie Haddow of West Perth that October.

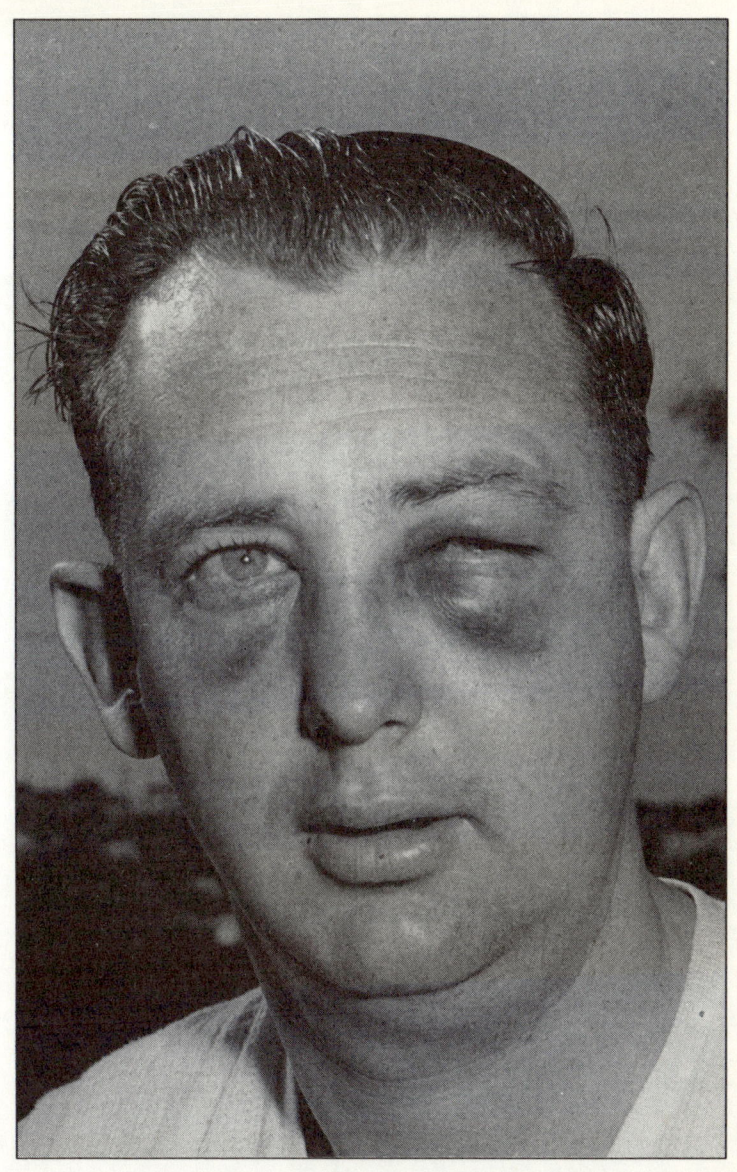

Wilson Onions and friends. (West Australian.)

The Goldfields National Football League in Western Australia has always been a pretty tough comp. The players are laconic and to the point, as highlighted in this *Football Record* excerpt of a charged player's tribunal evidence circa 1965.

'There was a scrum ... I was getting away to follow the progress of play ... I got a clout behind the ear ... looked around ... Miller was behind me ... so I clouted him'.

A remarkable piece of understatement is to be found in the GNFL minutes book of 1974 which simply states that a Noresman player was reported for striking Railways' players numbers 3, 4, 7, 10, 13, 14, 18, 20, and the Railways club secretary during the half-time break.

The 1982 GNFL Grand Final provided Railways captain-coach Neville Brierley with a notorious 197th and (temporarily) last game of a long career. His team lost the flag but won the fights with Brierley leading from the front and being reported on several occasions. The tribunal verdict was: 6 weeks for striking K Dale, 8 weeks for head-butting W Forrest, 6 weeks for striking W Forrest, 8 weeks for head-butting G Lightfoot and 6 weeks for striking G Lightfoot — in all 34 weeks of suspension. The tenacious Brierley served his sentence and returned to play in 1985.

BLOOPERS BY UMPIRES AND LEAGUE OFFICIALS

CHUMPIRES

THE WORST UMPIRING DECISIONS

Umpires. Every time our team loses we want to place them in a coffin that has sharp spikes dripping from its lid, we want to drop them into a used-auto compress and pull the lever, we want to take that whistle and shove it where it will play like a tuba.

What a sad and boring place the Hall Of Shame would be if it was devoid of umpires!

For this reason we bring the following incidents to your attention.

1947 WAFL GRAND FINAL
SOUTH FREMANTLE V WEST PERTH

In the 1947 WAFL Grand Final South Fremantle were trailing West Perth by 3 points in the last quarter. As West's Alwyn Whittle was kicking for goal, South tough guy Frank 'Scranno' Jenkins whacked Jack Larcombe behind the play — right in front of the public grandstand. Whittle's kick went through for a major, but umpire MICK CRONIN, having seen Jenkins' effort, brought the ball back to where the incident occurred. South cleared the ball and went on to win the match.

In another South Fremantle match Cronin paid a free kick against South and rover Steve Marsh called him a 'bald-headed old bastard'. After the game Cronin joined the South players for a beer at the Freemasons Hotel. Before Marsh had time to blink Cronin had smacked him across the chops. 'Just you watch who you call a "bald-headed old bastard",' commanded the umpire.

1899 East Fremantle and West Perth were playing the game that would decide the Premier. East's Mick Kenny had marked well within kicking distance when time was called. The shot would normally be a 'gimme' but the pigskin must have been purchased from a gypsy on the high seas because the ball had been slowly deflating.

Being the bad-sports they were, West Perth refused to allow Kenny to have a replacement ball. His shot reached the goal line but did not cross — West Perth won the game and the flag by 4 points. One can only ask why the ump didn't go the pump!

WHITE LINE THIEVER

In 1979 while Jon English was topping the charts and starring in *Against The Wind*, COLLINGWOOD and CARLTON were set to meet in a Grand Final.

As it happened, the game was one of the best Grand Finals of the modern era.

First Collingwood asserted their superiority, then Carlton came back only to face another Collingwood surge. As the game hung in the balance, Carlton's Wayne Harmes threw himself at a ball rolling over the boundary line, and in one of the great acts of football desperation knocked the ball back into play, setting up Ken Sheldon to score the decisive goal.

Replays showed the ball had been out of bounds.

Okay, the ump didn't have a video replay unit, it happened in a fraction of a second and Harmes' effort maybe deserved to be rewarded but all the same, Collingwood were stifferooned on that one and given another 11 years to wait for flag time.

CLASSIC CASES WHERE THE FIELD UMPIRE WAS IN THE WRONG

Richmond's full-back MAURIE SHEAHAN was the victim of some dud umpiring when opposed to Bob Pratt. In a close game, Sheehan went to kick a placekick after South Melbourne had scored a point. The umpire ruled he was deliberately wasting time and handed the ball over to Pratt who promptly goaled. The VFL later overruled the ump's decision saying the ball was not in play.

In a game at Perth Oval in 1978 BARRY CABLE, then captain-coach of East Perth, spun a web around the field umpire.

East Fremantle's legendary full-back Brian Needle (legendary because of his ability to make the most spectacular of errors) kicked off from a behind but the umpire ruled he had overstepped the goal line and prepared to bounce the ball as stipulated in the rules.

Cable appeared on the scene and somehow not only convinced the umpire that East Perth should receive a free kick, but that he should take it!

The umpire compounded and Cable goaled setting up a good win for his team.

GOAL CHUMPS

A number of goal umpires have inducted themselves into the Hall Of Shame with wrong decisions but not all have the misfortune to have their mistake captured on film.

In the Collingwood–Footscray clash of 1995 a shot from DERMOTT BRERETON quite clearly went through for a behind, but the goal umpire signalled full points.

When Footscray's Brownlow Medallist Tony Liberatore commented that the decision was a disgrace and the umpire should not be given another league game, he led his club to being fined $1500.

UMPIRES WHO DIDN'T QUITE MAKE IT

COWARD OF THE COUNTY

Though not a regular occurrence, it does happen that umpires get knocked out or injured during a game. For it to happen in a Grand Final though is noteworthy. Poor umpire Coward had the disappointment of not being able to complete the 1939 Grand Final. In the 2nd term the man in white tripped over in a bunch of players and dislocated his elbow. Play continued for a time with Melbourne even kicking a goal which could not be officially scored as Coward was unable to give the all clear. Coward had to leave the field and the emergency ump take over.

Coward though did better than South Australian umpire Norden. In 1907 Norwood and Port played at such a relentless pace that Norden suffered a minor heart attack and had to be replaced.

UMPIRES OF DUBIOUS CHARACTER

We can't actually say we have umpires who were cheats, though we'd be foolish to think it had never happened in the history of the game. Certainly there were allusions to it in the game's early years.

In 1886 a big rift at Norwood saw Topsy Waldron, upon being replaced as captain, accuse a club founder, Mr Henry Charles Burnet, of 'excessive fraternisation' with umpires. The club stood by Burnet, and Waldron later made his peace with the club.

GEORGE TOPPING was a lightly built Carlton player with a quick temper. In 1910 he was suspended for the rest of the year and for all of 1911. In 1912 he played a single game then in 1913 joined the VFA as a field umpire. One can only imagine that players were most respectful of his decisions.

'BECAUSE WE SAY SO'
THE MOST SHAMEFUL DECISIONS BY LEAGUE OFFICIALS

It's not just umpires who can make a shameful and shakey decision.

Sometimes a governing body has to make difficult decisions on the basis of what's good for the game. Just occasionally, the final decision is not based on any sense of logic, compromise or negotiation. It is simply an ultimatum from a bully body to what it considers its 'fag'. On other occasions club jealousies override fairness as a consideration, leading to rulings that could never be brought down by an impartial court. The following incidents are hereby inducted into the Hall Of Shame:

WAFL PREMIERSHIPS 1905 AND 1907

In 1905, 6 years after East Fremantle and West Perth were involved in a controversial premiership decider (*see EMPTY BLADDER*), the same two clubs were once again at it. In the decider, when time was called the scoreboard showed East winning by a point 6.5 to 5.10. Ten minutes later the goal umpires declared a draw saying their cards agreed but did not tally with the scoreboard.

The league refused East Fremantle's request to produce independent witnesses who could account for each of the scoring shots.

West won the replay and the flag.

Perhaps the league was right to back the umpires. After all what the umpire says is right, right? No — at least not in the West at the turn of the century.

In 1907 East Fremantle were once again victims of a disputed score. The Grand Final scoreboard showed East 6.11 beating Perth 6.6. Perth however protested a goal kicked by Charles Doig before half-time. Doig had marked, the bell had gone and umpire Crapp had quite rightly awarded Doig the chance to kick. His placekick sailed through for full points. Perth protested and the board upheld it!

Perhaps the decisions had more to do with the fact that East Fremantle had won every premiership between 1900 and 1907 except for those mentioned!

WEST COAST EAGLES V FOOTSCRAY
BRAWL 1994

The brawl was no heavyweight as brawls go, which is why it doesn't make the FOOTBRAWLS section of DOG DAY AFTERNOONS.

Danny Southern got Peter Sumich in a headlock and Sumich nearly choked, a couple of woolly punches were thrown and there was a bit of shoving.

It was what happened next that earned a place in the Hall Of Shame.

As was the usual procedure, the AFL's investigations officer Max Croxford looked at videotape to decide whether anybody ought to be charged. But this had both clubs on edge as the finals began the next week and both sides were participating.

Both breathed big sighs of relief though when Croxford determined no player had a case to answer.

Really, the matter should have ended there but in the meantime the AFL operations director, Ian Collins, had apparently told the clubs that any outcome might see them fined but no players charged.

The other AFL commissioners ruled that this sort of deal was not possible and eventually 4 players from each club were charged.

Footscray took out an injunction to prevent the case being heard until they had played their Qualifying Final and the Eagles also threatened legal action.

Finally both clubs abandoned that road and fronted up. All players were cleared in the hearing, thus ending a tacky episode that eroded confidence in all aspects of the league's judicial process.

1935 SANDOVER MEDAL

When in 1935 Lou Daily and George Krepp tied for the Sandover Medal, the league president, forgetting the system had changed, awarded Daily the medal on his casting vote. When Krepp's club, Swan Districts, pointed out that Krepp was the rightful winner on count back, the league reversed the decision. Krepp, to his honour, refused to accept the medal in this fashion and both players were awarded a medal.

CONTROVERSIAL PERSONALITY: RAY MONTGOMERY

It is doubtful whether any umpire or referee of any sport in Australia has managed to quite stamp themselves on the sport the way Ray Montgomery did in the WAFL during a flamboyant career that spanned 3 decades.

Montgomery's controversial tenure of the whistle saw him report many of the greatest players of the era and make his own name as known as any of the great players.

It is whispered that one disgruntled player once tried to run the umpire over in the car park after the game.

At least two players tried to make him the victim of an on-field collision, and at one memorable tribunal appearance the great East Fremantle and East Perth player and coach, Jack Sheedy, wanted to swear on the bible that he was innocent of Monty's charges.

Between 1955 and 1974 Monty laid 68 charges against 59 players and 1 trainer resulting in 55 convictions for total suspensions of 116 weeks and 5 pounds in fines.

The number of charges Montgomery laid against players and officials, by club, were: South Fremantle (16), East Fremantle (15), East Perth (11), West Perth (8), Subiaco (5), Swan Districts (5), Perth (4), Claremont (4)

Monty even once laid a charge against East Perth coach Jack Sheedy for criticising his umpiring in a newspaper article. The charge was dismissed, as was East Perth's countercharge against the umpire.

Montgomery's image might have been that of a report-happy ump wetting the pencil lead as he bounced the ball, but given the number of games he umpired, he does not, in fact, appear to have been overly zealous.

Even as advisor to the umpires at the WAFL tribunal, Monty could not escape controversy. After Mal Brown copped 6 weeks for striking West Perth's Leon O'Dwyer with an elbow, Monty claimed that Brown had assaulted him outside the tribunal. Nothing came of the incident.

If you believe that the best umpire is the one you don't notice then Monty is a definite Hall Of Shame candidate. On the other hand, if you believe that an umpire should be immune to verbal or physical threat from players, then a number of the players and officials booked over the years must head shamefacedly towards the Hall.

FOOT IN MOUTH
MEDIA MUCK-UPS AND COMMENTARY
CATASTROPHES

Given the pace of the game it's a wonder there aren't more slips from the commentary box.

When TED WHITTEN called Geelong's Darren Forseman, 'Darren Foreskin', nobody was sure whether it was deliberate or not, but West Australian ARTHUR MARSHALL'S misnaming of Benny Vigona as 'Benny Vagina' definitely was a mistake. So was TIM FLYNN'S contemptuous rebuff of a Sydney Swan who had just made a glaring mistake, 'He should be wanked off now!' yelled Flynn.

Many a commentator has noted that after a particularly spectacular piece of play 'the cloud stood up and crapped'.

7's SANDY ROBERTS made the international bloopers' arena when he introduced a beauty queen as 'Leanne Cock' instead of Leanne Dick.

One of the more unusual commentator prat-falls was that of the legendary GEORGE GRLJUSICH (6WF). George, an avowed South Fremantle supporter, was calling a South game and noted a particularly fine mark by a young South Fremantle player. 'Who is that player?' he asked his co-commentator.

'That's Rod Grljusich,' came the reply.

George had failed to recognise his own son.

This pales though compared to George's efforts in 1995 when George found his beloved Fremantle Oval press-box cluttered with community radio callers from 100FM. As the match was a derby, George was naturally more upset than he would normally be — and those that know George know that 'normally' would be about 9 on the aggro scale. In an article in the *Fremantle Herald* (22 April 1995) Brian Mitchell noted that the *Herald*'s source claimed Grljusich had been shouting obscenities, kicking boxes, leads and cables, and attempting to uproot the top of the ABC-TV counter. Grljusich played down his role when interviewed by Mitchell. He said that he attempted calm persuasion, but the 100FM callers were disinclined to move and he ended up thumping the table, but not their equipment.

Said Grljusich to Mitchell, '100FM is a very unimportant broadcasting organisation. This is the crux of your story, the crux of your story isn't my personality and characteristics. Those chookf...ers weren't going to move. Those blokes with social science degrees don't like being told by a balding guru like myself that "Boys, you shouldn't be here".'

As Mitchell noted, then came the comment that best of all explained George's attachment to that territory.

'In 1961 I had intercourse on the counter exactly where their equipment was. I can remember her name — Julie — she's still alive.'

The Grljusich–100FM imbroglio was small potatoes compared to what happened at Waverly Park in the early 80s when TONY BANKS and RICHARD DEMIAN came to blows in a dispute over a press-box seat.

Occasionally the media are on the receiving end of a player or coach's frustrations. Melbourne reporters found themselves dodging TONY LOCKETT'S crutches after he had sought treatment at a hospital following a game injury. Perth reporter CHRIS WOODS had his microphone ripped apart by an angry MAL BROWN, while the *Sun*'s DARYL TIMMS was manhandled by MICK MALTHOUSE. That incident occurred after the close game in which Essendon had pipped the Eagles with virtually the last kick of the day, and Kevin Sheedy had taken to whirling his jacket above his head.

DENNIS COMMETTI, Channel 7 commentator, past West Perth player and coach, and radio DJ, had the shame of being sprung paying for a hoarding at the oval advertising himself! Perhaps Den felt he needed something to make people forget this early photo.

Kick along with
Dennis Commetti –

6KY NA

MON-THURS, SAT., 7 p.m. - Midnight
SUN, 10 a.m. - 2 p.m.

DOOM RECRUITS

ALL-TIME DUD TRADES

This section is reserved especially for those recruiting personnel and officials who in attempting to pave their club with gold manage only to smear it in lemon. For seabed, Mindinao Trench-depth of dud deals, these take some beating.

JOHN PITURA FOR FRANCIS JACKSON, BRIAN ROBERTS AND GRAEME TEASDALE

In 1975 ABBA were roaring up the charts, flares were the acme of fashion and South Melbourne's John Pitura was the hottest property since St Paul's Cathedral in the Great Fire of London. Richmond wanted Pitura but South weren't about to let the ex-Wagga boy go without extracting the sort of deal that made Maverick smile. Richmond dealt a joker, a jack and an ace. The joker was the enormously popular Brian 'Whale' Roberts whose clubmanship was worth as much as his on-field bulk. The jack was Francis Jackson. In 100 games for South he was tough and dependable. The ace was Graeme Teasdale who won a Brownlow in 1977 — the year he also won Swans Best and Fairest. Teasdale played 122 games for the Red and Whites and twice topped their goal kicking. Pitura played 40 games for Richmond before exiting in 1977 to coach in Sydney.

NEVILLE FIELDS FOR TERRY AND NEALE DANIHER

Like a lot of gamblers who fluke a jackpot, the Swans recruiting staff began to think they actually knew what they were doing. They took all their John Pitura winnings and let them ride on their next deal. In 1978 they swapped brothers Terry and Neale Daniher to Essendon for the Dons' silky skilled centre-man Neville Fields. They lost.

Terry Daniher, who in his 19 games for South had shown lots of potential, wound up playing 294 games and kicking 449 goals for the Bombers. He captained Victoria and Australia in Ireland, captained Essendon to flag wins, won the goal kicking and the Best and Fairest. Neale Daniher played 82 games for Essendon before a terrible knee injury stopped his career. Fields was a serviceable player for South Melbourne, but no more. He finished his career back at Essendon.

IAN STEWART FOR BILL BARROT

On the face of it, it seemed a reasonable swap. Bill Barrot was a top centreman in Richmond's 1967 and 1969 flag sides who wanted out of Punt Road, Ian Stewart had won two Brownlows at Moorabbin but was sick of the Saints. It should have worked out okay for everyone. But it wouldn't be football if the Saints got the better end of the bargain. Stewart started with Richmond the year Silver Knight won the Melbourne Cup and finished when Harry White and Think Big grabbed the first of their two. Barrot was in and out of the Saints before the paint on his locker had dried. Stewart played 78 games at his new club, Barrot 2. Stewart won his third Brownlow and played in the Tigers' '73 flag side. Barrot tried out as a punter in the USA.

Given the Pitura, Fields and Barrot experience one can only offer this word of caution to recruiting officers: Beware the long striding centre-men, they will get you every time.

GERALD MCCARTHY FOR TERRY WALLACE

Round about the time Dragon were singing about Cuba and Sunshine, Fitzroy decided to lash out and get a champion. A few whip-rounds in Gore Street, a couple of quinellas on the Bundeena dogs and the Roys managed to come up with

171

$15,000 and an untried player for Hawthorn's Gerald McCarthy. McCarthy's steady if unspectacular service to Fitzroy (75 games) did not quite match that of the untried player passed over to Hawthorn. That was Terry Wallace who racked up 254 league games with Hawthorn, Richmond and Footscray. He played in 3 flag sides, represented Victoria 3 times and won 2 Best and Fairests with the Hawks and 2 more with the Dogs.

RUSSELL GREENE FOR MARK SCOTT AND TONY KING

In 1980 St Kilda swapped Russell Greene to Hawthorn for Tony King and Mark Scott.

Greene was given no prior knowledge of the deal, he trained with the Saints on the Thursday and stripped for the Hawks 2 days later.

Greene didn't know it then, but he was luckier than Claudia Schiffer's mattress.

For St Kilda he had played 120 games. He added 184 more at Hawthorn, won the Hawks Best and Fairest in 1984, captained Victoria and played in Hawthorn's 1983, 1986 and 1988 premiership teams.

Tony King played just 4 games at the Saints while Mark Scott kicked 110 goals in his 34 games before moving on to Fitzroy. He twice topped the Saints' goal kicking (48 goals 1980 and 45 goals 1982). If only he'd have had Russell Greene playing up the ground, Scott might have developed into a very good forward!

WILLIAM MORRIS FOR C GALBRAITH

Morris played 1 game in the Melbourne reserves before joining the army (1940). Jack Dyer liked the look of Morris and managed to get him to Tigerland where he played 141 games and kicked 89 goals. In his 1st full year (1945) he won the Best and Fairest and played for Victoria. He won the Brownlow in 1948, the only year of his career he did not represent his State. In fact he captained the 1950 Carnival side, won his 3rd Best and Fairest and finished second in the Brownlow that year. Galbraith played just 4 games for Melbourne before injury finished his career. Incredibly, one of these two players suicided in 1960 — Morris, the man who had the great career, could not stand to go on at the age of 38.

GEOFF RAINES TO COLLINGWOOD

After winning the Tigers Best and Fairest 1978, 1980 and 1981, Raines was traded to Collingwood in 1983 for $200,000 and three players: Neil Peart, Wally Lovett and Terry Domburg.

He left in 1987 after 47 games when he refused to accept a pay cut.

THE ROSS LYON AFFAIR

RON JOSEPH has often been credited as the man who took 100lbs of clay and made the North Melbourne fans' lives worth living.

Actually it wasn't clay but dollars that Joseph used to bring champions to Arden Street.

Exploiting the new 'ten-year rule' under which veteran players could ditch their old club, and with an astute interstate recruiting spree, Joseph turned North from easybeats to beat-ya-easys.

The Kangas won their first two flags ever with Joseph at the helm, making him the first administrator to be as famous as the players he signed. When the AFL wanted to lift Sydney from the bottom of the harbour, the salvage operator they went for was Mr Joseph. With old mate Barassi bedded down as coach and improving the Swans little by little, Joseph helped lure Tony Lockett and Paul Roos northwards. The Swans were on a roll. But then Ronny J crapped out.

In the 1995 March draft the Swans had earmarked ex-Fitzroy defender Ross Lyon as the number 1 pick. Trouble was, the AFL said Lyon would break the Swans salary cap. Lyon was bypassed and picked up by the Bears.

The omelette landed on Ron Joseph's face and he resigned.

Maybe he wanted out anyway. The mess-up was embarrassing but minor in relation to the recruiting positives he'd brought to the club.

What's more, Lyons, who was picked up by Brisbane, copped a severe injury missing all of '95.

At the time of writing Lyons looks unlikely to ever play again.

INTERSTATE DISAPPOINTMENTS

Anybody in the entertainment industry will tell you that no matter what rules you follow, no matter what worked last time, getting a top-ten recording or blockbuster film is still a matter of chance. Recruiting interstate footballers is very much like that. Some players who are giants in one State just don't make it when they move. Perhaps conditions don't suit their style of play, perhaps they miss the lifestyle or family or their home town, perhaps they left it too late or perhaps they weren't that good after all. Often they are resented by team-mates or coaches and never given a fair go.

Some players, having been champions in their own State and finding themselves duds in their adopted town, transfer back to once again become champions. These teams are therefore only related to performance of players as 'recruits' and not over the course of their career.

FB	Clinton Browning (EF to HAW to FOOT)	Ray Holden (WP to MEL)	Bert Thornley (EF to CAR)
HB	Shane Ellis (EF to ESS)	Stephen Hargreave (PERTH to FOOT)	Brad Shine (SD to CAR)
C	Bill Valli (WP to COLL)	J Parkinson (CL to COLL)	Graeme Heal (SUB to NM)
HF	Mario Turco (EF to NM)	Max George (SD to FITZ)	Barry Day (WP to ESS)
FF	Gary Shaw (QLD to CL to COLL)	Graeme Scott (SF to ST K)	Steve Malaxos (CL to HAW)
RK	Rhett Bayens (P to CA)	Steve da Rui (EP to CAR)	Peter Spencer (EP to NM)

Interchange from: Kevin Taylor (EF to SM), Tom Marinko (EP to ST K), Greg Jones (SD to ST K), Mick Jez (EF to ST K to CAR), Craig Hoyer (SD to Haw), Paul Gow (SD to FOOT), Gerard Neesham (EF to S), Dan Foley (WP to RIC), Mark Bayliss (SF to COLL), Brett Yorgey (P to COLL), M Wrensted (EF to WC to COLL), Willie Dick (P to ESS).

Many of the above players were pretty much unknown quantities when they went East but some left as Sandover Medallists and State players.

PETER SPENCER had won a Sandover Medal at East Perth but was unable to get up to the pace of VFL football. He went back to Perth and won a 2nd Sandover in 1984, tying with STEVE MALAXOS who couldn't get a regular game at Hawthorn, but who won the Eagles' inaugural Best and Fairest 2 years later when allowed to play as a centre-man-ball getter/distributor instead of as a receiver-attacker.

MURRAY WRENSTED was another whose physical characteristics and skills were similar to Greg Williams, but who was never given the chance at AFL level to play in a suitable position.

JOHN PARKINSON won a surprise Sandover in one very good year, but was already off the boil when he went to an even hotter competition.

PHIL NARKLE and PHIL KELLY were Sandover Medallists who don't quite make the list. Both were wingmen who showed something of their ability at St Kilda and North Melbourne respectively, but still fell well short of expectations.

DUDS FROM THE SOUTH TO THE EAST

FB	Neil Hein (NOR to BRIS)	Jim Tilbrook (STURT to MEL)	Michael Parsons (NA to SWANS)
HB	Greg Whittelsea (STURT to HAW)	Andrew Bennett (SA to HAW to ST K)	Russel Ebert (PORT to NM)
C	Glynn Hewitt (WA to RICH)	Robert Day (WA to HAW)	Dominic Fotia (TORRENS to CAR)
HF	Grant Fielke (WA to COLL)	Damien Kitschke (SA to ST K)	Milan Faletic (SA to ST K)
FF	Adam Garton (GLEN to BRIS)	Jim West (GLEN to SWANS)	Graham Cornes (GLEN to NM)
RK	Dean Farnham (CD to FITZ)	Graham Molloy (SA to MEL)	Anthony Antrobus (NA to ESS to ST K)

Interchange from: Mark Weideman (WA to COLL), Seth Parry (WA to FITZ), Daryl Hewitt (WOOD to RICH to ST K), Bert Johnson (WA to NM), Jeff Bray (WA to SA), Bruce Lindner (WA to GEEL), Don Roach (WA to HAW), David Young (SA to SM to COLL), Candles Thompson (to HAW), Max James (PA to SM).

RUSSEL EBERT and GRAHAM CORNES probably went too late in their careers, but one wonders if a different coach may have made a difference. In his book *Crackers*, Crackers Keenan declared JIM TILBROOK as one of his great disappointments. Tilbrook though was never used the way he was by Sturt. Most of the others never reached the heights they did in

South Australia where the game was much more mark and kick until the 80s.

DUDS FROM THE EAST TO THE WEST

Players who nosedived in the West after coming from South Australia or Victoria.

FB	**Brendan McFaull**	**Noel Mugavin**	**Len Halley**
	(HAW to SU)	(FITZ to WP)	(ESS to WP)
HB	**Darryl Griffiths**	**Kevin O'Keefe**	**Peter Keayes**
	(ST K to CL)	(FITZ to EP)	(FITZ to EF)
C	**David Rhodes**	**Bruce Tschirpig**	**Graeme Schultz**
	(FITZ to SUB)	(RICH to EF)	(ESS to SUB)
HF	**Neville Fields**	**Roch Devenish-Meares**	**Corey Young**
	(ESS to EF)	(HAW to SU)	(RICH to WCE)
FF	**Damien Nygard**	**Darryl Sutton**	**Vin Catoggio**
	(NOR to WP)	(NM to SD)	(CAR to SU)
RK	**Bill Joiner**	**Ken Newlands**	**Mark Norsworthy**
	(HAW to EF)	(GEEL to EF)	(CD to EF)

Interchange from: Chris Mitchell (GEEL to EP), Dean Herbert (to P), Bill Byron (VFA to C), Robert Greenwood (ESS to C), Peter May (SA to SD).

Many of these players were not suited to Western Australian conditions: BRENDON McFAULL, LEN HALLEY and BILL JOINER lacked the mobility necessary on the bigger WA grounds where play was transferred quickly over fast surfaces.

NEVILLE FIELDS, KEN NEWLANDS and DARRYL GRIFFITHS came too late and many of the others seemed only to play in bursts.

FOOTY'S KINDLING

Ever been watching a game and seen a player take a series of towering marks, make dazzling dummies, kick superb goals on the run and from the pocket, and thought the new Jesaulenko, Whitten or Skilton has arrived? Then found yourself watching in vain for the rest of the game, season or player's career for the player to consistently display the skills he so obviously possesses? Such players are footy's kindling: they burn ever so brightly but never warm up the house. When the ice is forming over your team's chances they are soggy and ineffective. Instead of leaving the fans and coach with a warm inner glow they leave them with frostbite. Below is a team of contemporary players who, for whatever reason, have fizzled over quite a few seasons rather than warmed their club through many a cold winter.

Troy Ugle	Bruce Lindner	Michael Murphy
(WC)	(GEEL, AD)	(NM, AD, BRIS)
David Strooper	J Fidge	Craig Devonport
(FITZ, SWANS)	(MELB, BRIS, ESS)	(ST K)
Matt Ryan	Russell Richards	Frank Marchesani
(COLL, SWANS)	(MEL)	(FITZ, CARL)
Rene Kink	G Excell	Darren Cuthbertson
(COLL, ESS)	(GEEL, FITZ)	(MEL)
Terry Keayes	John Hutton	Scott Hodges
(COLL, RICH)	(BRIS, SYD, FTLE)	(AD)

Interchange from: Chris Mitchell (GEEL), Vin Catoggio (CARL, MELB, SYD), Silvio Foschini (SM, ST K), Russell Jeffrey (ST K, BRIS), Gary Keane (FITZ), Peter Kiel (ST K), Simon Meehan (ST K), Lee Murnane (FITZ), David Young (SM, COLL).

MAGNESIUM FLARE

Burning even faster and brighter than kindling some careers are bright magnesium flares, lighting up the landscape before plunging us back into dark. It might be war or injury that is the cause. Sometimes weaknesses become exploited by opponents, sometimes players can't handle the fame, sometimes there is no logical explanation. The ability that has dazzled thousands vanishes into some Bermuda triangle beneath the oval. It is a great FOOTBALL SHAME that for whatever reason these players were unable to carve a long career as brilliant as their debut.

The Richmond outfit of 1920 had not one but two such supernovas.

GEORGE OGILVIE played just 2 games. His debut was described by John Worrall as the best he had ever seen. On the eve of the Grand Final he was ruled ineligible for Richmond because on his registration statement he had claimed to have been in the army for 3 years when in reality it was 2 years 9 months.

WILLIAM JAMES came into the 1920 Grand Final team for his 1 and only game when star full-forward Bayliss was ill. He kicked the goal that sealed the flag and played in the flag side for Kyabram the same week. During a hunting trip the following summer his companion's gun shot him in the foot and he never played again.

Another Richmond disappointment, ruckman GARY WILLIAMSON (Richmond, 1960-4 and South Melbourne, 1965: 43 games total), looked to be a real find in 1961 but his career never took off and he wound up at South Melbourne.

Hawthorn have had a trifecta of players who 'might-have-been'.

TERRY INGERSOLL, 1957-8, who won the Hawks' Best First-Year Player trophy returned to Sydney in 1959.

MICHAEL COOKE, in his debut, the 1975 Second Semi-final, kicked 4 goals and had everybody thinking he was the next Peter Hudson. He failed to kick a goal when Hawthorn were beaten by North in the Grand Final and never played senior footy again.

GLENN HOWARD (Hawthorn, 1981, 1983 and 1986; Collingwood, 1987: 37 games total) was a winger who looked like he could be anything but never quite made it after a series of severe injuries.

Naturally the Saints have had their share of flaming comets.

MILAN FALETIC (1981-2). St Kilda thought they had it all together when their South Australian recruit kicked 5 goals on debut. He played only 24 games in all with 33 goals total.

WILLIAM LINGER (1953-4) came 2nd in the Best and Fairest in his first year but played only 31 games, 12 fewer than NEVILLE LINNEY (1953-7) who made the State side after just a handful of games on the half-back flank.

Back in 1939, KEVIN O'HALLORAN kicked 7 goals in his first game but played just 7 games with St Kilda, 2 with South Melbourne and 5 with Footscray.

Other Magnesium Flares include:

PETER FALCONER (Geelong, Carlton) who polled 11 Brownlow votes in 14 games in his 1st year but after just 20 games crossed to Carlton for 24 more.

LOU DAILY (Collingwood, Geelong 1933-34,) kicked 10 goals on debut and only 18 in the other 18 games he played.

Half-forward flanker MARK DWYER (Fitzroy 1986-7,) polled 10 Brownlow votes in his first year. But after 13 games with the Roys he crossed to the Saints in 1988 for just 1 game.

ALLAN JENNINGS (Footscray, 1982) had a career of 9 games for 15 goals. He kicked 5 in each of his first 2 games and the Dogs' fans must have thought they had at last found the Messiah.

A skinny rover, CHARLES PAGNOCOLLO (1970-73 —

Footscray: 46 games; Melbourne: 1) was believed by many to be a potential superstar after his first year. He failed to live up to the promise.

Another lithe player was MATTHEW RYAN (1985-92 — Collingwood, Sydney, Brisbane). Ryan was runner up in the Copeland Medal in 1987, but from there is was all downhill.

THE OTHER BROTHER

Sometimes whole families are blessed with natural (genetic) sporting skill that is only enhanced by intra-familial games.

But genes can be cruel, especially in the case of footballing brothers. There are those lucky sets of brothers where abilities are matched or complementary. Often though, only one brother ever is good enough to play league football. That's probably not so unfair to the non-footballing brother. Instead of running up sandhills he gets on with his life making millions or spending time with his family.

But in some unfortunate cases a brother is good enough to play league but at nowhere near the level of his champion brother. He goes through the pain without the gain. There is no shame in being the lesser brother — as pointed out often enough in this book, at least they've been good enough to play at the top level. The only shame is that they weren't as good as their brother.

Imagine if these two teams of brothers lined up on one another! (In brackets are the number of AFL/VFL games, followed by the number of goals kicked.)

F Kevin Ablett (37-22) *GARY ABLETT (216-659)	David Kernahan (53-8) *S KERNAHAN (231-961)	Ralph Rose (23-9) BOB ROSE (152-214)
HF Daryl Cunningham (41-32) G.CUNNINGHAM (224-58)	Don Whitten (24-1) TED WHITTEN (321-364)	Steve Richardson (1-2) M RICHARDSON (156-174)
C Larry Watson (35-2) TIM WATSON (307-337)	Jay Viney (23-4) *TODD VINEY (160-61)	D Schimmelbusch (48-27) W SCHIMMELBUSCH (306-355)
HF Peter Worsfold (31-24) *JOHN WORSFOLD (176-35)	Scott Spalding (1-0) *EARL SPALDING (195-151)	Tom Flower (26-28) R FLOWER (272-315)
FF Gerard Toohey (1-0) BERNARD TOOHEY (267-116)	Graeme Cordy (27-9) NEIL CORDY (236-31)	Kevin Rush (7-4) BOB RUSH (146-1)
RK Craig Balme (3-0) NEIL BALME (159-229)	Paul Atkins (2-0) *SIMON ATKINS (149-83)	Graham Osborne (37-10) *R OSBORNE (244-535)

Interchange:

Graeme Peck (31-13) JOHN PECK (213-475)	Robert Briedis (9 -0) A BRIEDIS (162-279)	Stuart Glascott (4-0) D GLASCOTT (173-81)

*still playing

With 9 Best and Fairest awards, nearly 4,500 games and 5,500 goals in their collective AFL/VFL careers one has to feel the STAR BROTHERS would inflict a hiding on the OTHER BROTHERS whose combined total of games (464) does not match any single line of the Stars. The OTHERS total of career goals (195) is bettered by every STARS line, except the full-back line!

NO FRILLS NO THRILLS

You'll often hear footy writers or coaches go on about 'no-frills' players.

This means players who kick like they have Parkinson's disease, couldn't sell a dummy in a maternity ward and display the flare of a country rec. centre.

The game's afficionadoe will tell you it doesn't matter that these players are more soporific than a handful of mogadons, the important thing is they get the ball.

And how right they are. Can you imagine the shiver that would travel down footy's backbone if ever these immortals lined up on one another?

THE VIC AND TASSIE SOWS' EARS V THE WEST AND SOUTH WILD BORES.
(SOWS EARS KICKING DOWN)

Sean Ralphsmith	Brian Winton	Lawrie Bingham
David Bain	Dean Farnham	John Ironmonger
Micky Gayfer	Dean Wallis	David Polkinghorne
Stephen Rowe	Michael O'Connell	Wayne Weideman
Des Meagher	Graeme Yeats	Jason Daniels
Gary Gillespie	Todd Viney	Peter Vertudaches

Peter Czerkaski	Robert Groenewegen	Adrian Burns
Eric Sarich	Darren Gaspar	Andrew Rogers
Brian Sierekowski	Dany Del Re	Michael Reeves
Ivan Glucina	Brian Needle	Simon Outhwaite
James Manson	Craig Potter	Greg Healy
Ian McCullough	Mark Zanotti	Dominic Fotia

Just look at some of the classic duels and how the ad men could promote with catchy slogans:

Polkinhorne v Weideman (TWO BEASTS NO BEAUTY)

Manson v McCullough (TWO HACKS IN SEARCH OF A WELTER)

Needle v Del Re (THE GOAL SQUARE'S IMMORTAL CHALLENGE: WILL BRIAN FUMBLE BEFORE DANNY STUMBLES)

Gayfer v Rowe (TWO MEN IN SEARCH OF A BOUNDARY LINE)

For half-time entertainment South Fremantle's Ivan Glucina could show us his party trick of putting a dozen eggs in one hand while Yeats, Daniels and Burns conducted kicking clinics for the youngsters.

You can guarantee this match would have crowds flooding through the turnstile into the oval: so long as this game was played in the streets!

AFTER HOURS

FOOTY PRANKERS

One of football's great joys are its practical jokes. Here are some footy pranks that induct the 'Prankees' into Footy's Hall Of Shame.

STEPHEN LUNN

Lunn was working for the Dogs in their offices and involved in that murky water called 'marketing' when his ears pricked up at a front desk enquiry. A Dogs' fan wanted to come and play with the team. Lunn's interest was aroused. He told the secretary that he would look after this potential Dogs' 'recruit' whom, given the subsequent events, we can only assume was one stud short of the full boot.

'So you want to join the Dogs?' asked Lunn.

Yes, the recruit felt he could make a difference.

'Okay, let's check your fitness.'

Lunn sent the recruit on a lap of the Oval. About halfway around the recruit was coughing and spluttering.

'Well, looks like your fitness is okay. Let's try your skills.'

There followed a practice session in which Lunn drilled hard torpedo punts at the would-be. With leather bruising every surface of the would-be's body, Lunn announced that this hurdle too had been passed.

'So far so good. Now we'll try your strength.'

A couple of hundred pounds was put on the bar and the would-be was almost throttled by the steel he was trying to lift.

'That's fine, too,' said Lunn. 'So far as I can see, you're in top shape. Okay, you're in the side. I want to see you at 3.00 pm Saturday on the back flank. Now go down to Jack Holland's sports store and get a Footscray jumper with number 15 on the back.'

The next Saturday the recruit ran onto the field at 3.00 pm

and lined up on his astonished opponent (it was a Hawthorn game and we think it might have been Peter Curran). At least the new Bulldog was both punctual and a tight checker — something many of his team-mates could have fruitfully copied.

When last seen the recruit, wearing jeans, footy boots and a new Footscray long-sleeved jumper with number 15 on the back, was being escorted from the ground by police.

JOCK BARTLETT

South Melbourne/Sydney Swans' trainer Jock Bartlett had an unpleasant surprise planned for new recruits. The enormously well-endowed Jock would cut a hole in the pocket of his jacket and position his 'flute' beneath the hole. Then on some pretext, he would get a raw recruit to reach into his (Jock's) pocket. As the ingenue recoiled in terror at what was lurking there, the change rooms shook with laughter.

It took some time, but finally the players got their own back on Jock. The team was staying at the Hawaii Hilton Village when a huge storm lashed the area and blacked out the hotel. The players called the trainer's room, one floor above, and impersonated the concierge. Jock was told that the storm had made all metal surfaces 'live' and that he should avoid touching anything metal. He was asked to go to the floor below, taking the stairs as the lifts were out, and warn the players. Should he encounter anybody on the way he was told to shout to them to evacuate.

Huddled in the dark the players waited to see if their plan worked. Finally the door opened, a white towel held over the door knob as 'protection' from electrocution. As soon as the players erupted in a chorus of laughs, Jock knew he had been had.

One of Wynne's innovations at Norwood was a Friday lunch during which anything was likely to happen. Once Wynne and one of his accomplices in crime made a goat soup. Wynne had made sure that the skin of the creature was kept. When they served the soup to their fellow diners they did not reveal the ingredients. The gourmets were asked to guess what they were. When they had all given their estimation, Wynne announced they had been eating dog.

The diners did not panic. Wynne was well known for his pranks.

'We don't believe you,' they said, in more colloquial language than that.

Wynne then produced the skin of the 'dog'. 'I knew you'd think that — proof!'

Like most pranksters, Wynn did not dish out pranks without being on the receiving end of a few himself. One, for which he held a particular grudge, may not have been deliberate, but in Wynne's eyes that didn't matter.

Wynne's great pal Ron Tremain ran the Old Lion pub. Through Tremain, Wynne got to meet Nat King Cole's brother, Ike. Ike was doing a season in Adelaide and got right into the football. When he heard Wynne expressing a desire to have a go at gridiron, Ike revealed he had a contact at the LA Rams and could get Wynne a tryout. Tremain thought this a good idea. The season was over, Wynne may as well go to LA. Tremain had the name of an agent contact that Wynne could stay with. So it was arranged.

Wynne flew into LA Airport, where the agent friend picked him up and announced that evening was Halloween and they would be attending a big Hollywood party. There was a catch though, you either had to come in fancy dress or go nude. Wynne decided his footy togs would pass as fancy dress and indeed they did cause much comment. The Aussie, who hadn't slept for some 24 hours, found the party a much needed eye-opener. The host and many of his guests frolicked nude in a giant pool and many interesting activities were on offer, including some pumpkin pie that was not 100% pumpkin.

Before long Wynne and the agent had found themselves two very attractive women and split for a more intimate atmosphere. Things were looking pretty good to the footballer when the girls asked them back to their place, but the agent was strict. John needed to rest.

As they sped away from the girls in the agent's convertible, Wynne protested that he really could have spent some more time with them.

'Plenty more of those,' offered his host, who then drove to his own pad.

They knocked back a few drinks, then the agent showed the footballer his room.

'I'll be just over here,' he said, indicating the adjacent room.

When the agent announced that his girlfriend was away for the week, Wynne began to hear faint warning bells.

He decided he would leave his footy shorts well and truly on.

Not long after lights out the agent called from his room.

'John, you feel like some sex?'

'Yea,' said Wynne, 'let's go back and find those sheilas we left.'

The agent clucked that he had something else in mind.

Wynne, already sleep-deprived for 36 hours, stayed awake all night not daring to drop off.

When Wynne returned to Adelaide it was time for a square-up with Tremain. At first Wynne was happy to push Tremain's car into no parking areas, where he kept getting tickets, but this seemed somehow unworthy as a payback. Wynne waited until they were flying to Alice Springs.

Gun-lover Tremain had packed his .303 and magnum, 'just in case'. At the airport Wynne asked a copper if it was legal for people to carry guns in their briefcase.

'Of course not.'

'Well I saw that bloke put guns in his,' said Wynne.

When two police came down the aisle and hoicked Tremain for an interview, payback was considered complete.

END OF REASON

THE NOTORIOUS END-OF-SEASON TRIP

The end-of-season jaunt is guaranteed to incorporate enough shameful behaviour to fill several CD-ROMs. Every Australian heading overseas dreads the day when he or she is scheduled on the same plane as a sporting club. That sporting blazer is almost diabolical in its ability to turn normally reasonable human beings into maniacal psychopaths. There are legendary stories of Bali and Bangkok bashes, but one trip stands out.

THE BULLDOG KENNEL IN THE FLYING KANGAROO

Footscray's end-of-season rates as the all-time Shamer. No other club has managed to achieve a worldwide ban by an airline.

The Dogs were flying Qantas from Australia to LA. The only management figure accompanying the team was coach Mick Malthouse, a major error by the club. The first leg, crewed by female attendants, took the team to Nandi. Aside from the usual hoonish high jinks, the trip was no great drama. Diminutive **TONY BUHAGIAR** had the team in stitches when he grabbed a flight attendant's jacket from a locker and followed behind the quarantine de-lousers spraying Rexona.

It was during the Nandi to Honolulu leg that things went awry. A couple of the senior players kept up an incessant commentary on the sexual preferences of the Qantas stewards, and it was this that was at the kernel of all subsequent problems. There were a few other incidents, such as Robert Gronewegen making an announcement over the PA for everybody to assume crash positions.

In those days the Qantas planes were each named after an

Australian city, and a small plaque at the back of the plane denoted it. Tony Buhagiar and his Sandgroper mates believed it auspicious that this particular plane was named 'Perth'. They removed the plaque from the plane as a souvenir; the given reason for the subsequent ban, although really just the flea that made the Kangaroo scratch. When the team landed in Honolulu, the captain requested that the team stay behind until other passengers had disembarked. Then the captain came down and announced that the plane would not carry the players beyond Honolulu. It was at this point that a team official would normally have made polite contrition and apologised on behalf of the team, but Malthouse was the most senior person on board and he was either ignorant of, or disinclined to take this action. Buhagiar and a couple of his accomplices were told they would not be carried further on the replacement flight and must return to Australia.

Things were to take a turn for the worse, however, when the Australian press got wind of the debacle. Qantas announced they would not honour the LA tickets at all and the team was 'put-off' in Honolulu. Using their own funds, the players organised accommodation on the island for a few days and then flew on to LA.

Eventually, after some negotiation, they flew back to Australia via Pan Am, completing the most SHAMEFUL trip in the history of Aussie sport.

NO NAMES NO PACK DRILL

In this section we recount some edifying stories concerning moments so SHAMEFUL that the identity of the protagonists must be kept concealed. Some stories were too racy to be included even with the cloak of annonymity. Perhaps at a later time they will be revealed in the sealed section of an X-rated publication. For now, these will have to satisfy your taste for scandal.

WANDERING PALMS

One football club in particular seems to have more than its share of foliage fanatics among its playing ranks.

One player spotted a couple of very nice tall palm trees that would just be the ants' pants in the backyard.

That they were actually the property of somebody else did not seem to matter or occur to this arbor enthusiast. He re-potted the palms and marvelled at the improvement to his property.

Some time later, during a barbecue at the verdant venue, one of the guests exclaimed to his green-thumbed host, 'You bastard, you're the one who took my palms!'

The special mark that had designated the palms' ownership was still there and it required some quick talking from the enthusiast and some familial blaming to save the day.

The same player had once before been forced to think on his feet while extricating jarrah woodwork from a bridge. A resident had seen what looked like untoward activity and come to investigate, but upon being assured that the 'maritime employees' were carrying out some maintenance, he was happy to assist with loading the wood into a vehicle.

Another player from the same club was also struck by the beauty of a large plant on a property not his own. He went back home, got the digger and removed the desired shrub. Unfortunately his criminal skills did not match his football skills and the trail of soil led direct to his place.

RULED UNFIT

It's not uncommon for players to be ruled unfit for the game at the very last minute by the team manager, but on one occasion a football manager had to actually rule himself out. The interstater had wreaked such havoc upon himself with some nocturnal 'fact finding' and 'scouting' missions in the strange city, that he declared himself out of the match. His fellow committeemen insisted he appear however, and so the club doctor was called in to give him a shot for temporary relief. Surely this is the only time that football manager has been given a painkiller to get him to the ground!

CARPET BURNS

The father of a young recruit came to the city to check out the digs the club provided for its young interstate and country recruits.

He was met by the football manager and taken on a guided tour of bathrooms, kitchen and so forth.

When they opened the door to one of the bedrooms they were confronted by one of the young lodgers and his girlfriend on the bedroom floor 'in flagrante delicto'.

The football manager was embarrassed and lost for words.

The father took it in his stride. 'I might move in here myself,' he said.

One interstate footballer escorted a 'young lady' home by taxi. The place was way out in woop woop and the player kissed and canoodled his new girl all the way, his expectations, and perhaps something more than his temperature, rising. At the end of the substantial cab fare the young lady disembarked while the player stayed to pay the fare. The cabby, safe with the cash in hand then warned the player that his date was in fact a 'he'.

The player stayed in the cab and the cabby copped the return fare as well.

That player showed more restraint than a SANFL player who, some years before, had not discovered the sex of his partner until they were in the sack.

'Oh well, too late now,' remarked the player.

A famous or infamous transvestite/transexual named Karen lived near 'Whale' Roberts' pub and snared many a famous sportsperson in her web. A number of high-profile West Indies' cricketers were particularly impressed by the tall, firm-busted woman.

One Richmond rookie was set-up by his mates. He was sent to Karen and some intimate moments followed.

When he rejoined his friends waiting in the bar he had quite a swagger.

The still-ignorant player thanked his friends for their efforts, who then dropped the bombshell.

'Pretty good for a bloke,' remarked the rookie, who then repaired for seconds.

Karen would conceal herself in bushes where the Richmond players would sprint first one way and then back. Legend has it that she would jump up and display her boobs. One player was notorious for winning the outward leg of the sprint so he could get a good look. Invariably he would be last on the way back.

On another occasion a Richmond player was drinking with a member of the rag trade when a familiar figure walked into the bar.

'Shit there's Karen,' said the player.

The other man looked over. 'I used to play with Karen when she was centre half-forward for Caulfield,' he said.

When Karen had enough of Richmond she began trawling Melbourne waters. Sir Billy Snedden was involved with the club at the time and Karen would continually ask Sir Billy for a lift home and promise some sexual favour in return. Sir Billy would politely decline.

Sir Billy died of a heart attack in a hotel room and rumour at the time placed a mysterious woman with him.

Presumably it was some uncharitable wag whose bereavement notice for Sir Billy read something like: 'Thanks for the good times — Karen'.

Swans — private edition.

GUESTS SHAME
SELECTIONS

JEFF RICHARDSON
COODABEEN CHAMPIONS

Doug Booth — for kicking a dog at Waverly
Ron Barassi — for the clothes he wore at the 1977 Grand
  Finals
Gerard Neesham — for declaring John Hutton to be the next
  Gary Ablett.

TONY DE BOLFO
HERALD SUN JOURNALIST

Tony Modra's magic word on 'Sportsworld'.
Scott Watters three-quarter time on-field leak.
The Millane-Banks bus hijack from Spencer Street station.
  (After missing the '91 Finals, Coolingwood's Darren
  Millane and Denis Banks, as a prank, and probably more
  than a little under the weather, attempted to hi-jack a bus full
  of passengers.)
The 'Battle Of Britain' between North Melbourne and Carlton.
  (An exhibition match held at The Oval, London, which
  degenerated into fisticuffs, with one player being shoved
  into a dustbin.)

H G NELSON
SPORTING LIFE AND CLUB BUGGERY LEGEND

When Peter Moore left Collingwood for Melbourne the
Collingwood cheer squad hung huge banners reading
'MOORE FILTH'.
Leigh Matthews for numerous fistic moments.

The song selection at the WAFL finals series of 1993 when
somebody decided that every space needed to be filled by
loud music. The play list was:

Elimination Final: half-time and three-quarter time — 'You
May Be Right' by Billy Joel.

Qualifying Final: pumping aerobics-type number at the 5
minute mark of the first quarter. (This was a mistake.)

First Semi-Final: half-time — 'Red Roses For A Blue Lady'
(singer unknown).

Second Semi-Final: half-time — 'Tonight, I Celebrate My
Love' by Peabo Bryson and Roberta Flack.

Three-quarter time — 'By The Time I Get To Phoenix' by
Glen Campbell.

Preliminary Final: pre-game — 'Chain Reaction' by Diana
Ross; 'La Bamba' by Los Lobos and 'Some People' by
John Farnham, which was cruelly interrupted by the
Subiaco club song. During the warm-up the disco version of
'You Keep Me Hanging On' was played.

BARRY CROCKER
ENTERTAINER, ACTOR

Barry Crocker, who (believe it or not) actually trained with the
Geelong thirds, nominated himself for the Footy Hall of
Shame.

He recalls flying in direct from the United States to sing at
the AFL Grand Final. 'Not many people know that I was the
first person to ever sing *Advance Australia Fair* at a Grand
Final,' he says.

'The sad thing was, the match was a draw.'

A lamenting Crocker had to return to the US, missing the
following weeks replay in which North Melbourne annihilated
Collingwood.

PETER WILSON
EAST FREMANTLE, RICHMOND AND W C EAGLES

Neville Crowe (ex-Richmond President) for eating flowers in front of his players at the London Hotel.

TIM FLYNN
BROADCASTER KICK FM

George Grljusich's stomping on his little red transistor radio at Fremantle Oval. The incident was building after commercial radio 'stole' George's preferred broadcast position. Then one of his horses must have lost for George pulled the earpiece from the tranny, threw it on the ground and jumped on it.

Also 'Clayton's Filth' — the Ron Boucher–Graham Moss clash in which Boucher emerged with a bloody gash across his cheek. The media beat it up as mild-mannered Moss exploding. Later Moss revealed that Boucher's own knee had done the damage.

SHIRLEY STRACHAN
ROCK STAR — TV AND RADIO PERSONALITY

The unprecedented criminal charging of Hawthorn legend Leigh Matthews after the breeze at Princes Park forced his elbow into contact with the jaw of Neville Bruns in the Hawthorn–Geelong game.

WILBUR WILD
TV PERSONALITY AND SAX FIEND

Those nitpicking pedants who made a thing of Daryl Braithwaite's AFL Grand Final version of 'Waltzing Matilda'. Sure Daryl had the swaggy jumping into the billabong about 3

times, and sure we never got the part about the squatter, but
Banjo's stuff is very long, and like all good pop singer's Daz
was just going for the lyric hook.

TONY BUHAGIAR
EAST FREMANTLE, ESSENDON, FOOTSCRAY

Kevin Sheedy for his secret strategy for beating Carlton. All
week we'd heard about it, then before the game, Sheed's
revealed secret ploy: Get Bruce Doull's headband and rip it
up. We couldn't believe this was the master strategy! Still,
when the opportunity arose and I saw the headband on the
ground, I remembered the coach's orders. Only thing is, have
you ever tried to rip a headband? In the end I had to throw it
into the crowd.

GREG CHAMPION
COODABEEN CHAMPIONS

Dave Granger for finals mayhem.
   (Granger played in South Australia, and in his last game, a
final, appeared to many to be a touch more interested in the
man than the ball — inspiring wide-spread debate on a send-
off rule.)

202

CLUB DUD

CLUB BY CLUB LOWLIGHTS

DROUGHTS

WAFL	SANFL	VFL/AFL
SUBIACO 48 (1925-72)	TORRENS 37 (1954-90)	STK 69 (1897-1965)
PERTH 47 (1908-54)	GLENELG 35 (1935-72)	SWANS 62 (1934-95)
STH FTL 29 (1918-46)	WST AD 32 (1937-71)	FITZ 51 (1945-95)
SWANS 27 (1934-60)	STH AD 32 (1900-34)	NTH M 50 (1925-74)
W PERTH 26 (1906-31)	STH AD 32 (1964-95)	FOOTS 41 (1955-95)
CLMNT 23 (1941-63)	CENTRAL 32 (1964-95)	HAW 36 (1925-60)
W. PERTH 19 (1976-94)	WOOD 27 (1964-90)	GEEL 32 (1964-95)
PERTH 18 (1978-95)	TORRENS 24 (1897-23)	MEL 31 (1965-95)
E PERTH 17 (1979-95)	STH AD 22 (1939-63)	COLL 31 (1959-89)
CLMNT 16 (1965-80)	STURT 22 (1941-65)	ST K 30 (1966-95)
STH FTL 16 (1900-15)	NORWOOD 24 (1951-74)	FOOT 29 (1925-53)
STH FTL 15 (1981-95)	STURT 19 (1977-95)	GEEL 26 (1897-25)
STH FTL15 (1955-69)	NTH AD 14 (1932-48)	RICH 23 (1944-66)

AFL/VFL CLUB LOWLIGHTS

(* denotes a record across all three major competitions.)

ADELAIDE

When Adelaide started most of the top South Australian players were bound to other AFL clubs. Gradually they got their act together before inexplicably falling away. People blame the one-club-in-town syndrome, they blame the coach and they blame the travel. We reckon you may as well blame the colours. How can you play commanding footy looking like a squashed licorice allsort? Time's running out for the Crows — Port have one foot in the AFL door. Maybe now the Grand Prix has gone the players will concentrate on their footy.

Percentage lost of all games played 52
Percentage of all finals lost 67
Worst flag drought 5 yrs, 91-95
Current flag drought 5 yrs
Longest losing sequence 4
Lowest score 4.7 v St K, 1991

OTHER SHAMEFUL EFFORTS

Adelaides's effort against the Swans in 1995 (*see WORST FADEOUTS*) when they kicked 1 point to 11 goals was highly shameful. The whopping 135-point hiding West Coast handed out in round 19, 1995, was another dark stain in Crowland.

When Adelaide beat St Kilda in round 18, 1995, it was their first win in Melbourne since defeating Hawthorn in 1993 at the MCG, and only their second win in Victoria in 25 trips.

The Crows' home crowd is even worse than Collingwood's.

DOOM RECRUITS

Tom Warhurst, Robert Thompson, Darren Smith, Adam Saliba, Stephen Rowe, Paul Paterson, Romano Negri, Clayton Lamb, Matthew Kelly.

BRISBANE

When the AFL took licence fees from Brisbane and Sydney without giving them the infrastructure they needed to support their teams in a hostile (rugby league) environment, it nominated itself for HALL OF SHAME status. Each of the Victorian clubs in the competition likewise inducted itself into the Hall Of Shame for the pathetic recruits they offered Brisbane. Carlton went so far as to offer players who had retired or were terminally injured. All the same, the Bears have not been idle in accruing their own Hall Of Shame credentials with their guernsey design (*see CRUD DUDS*) and their recruiting being particularly Bare.

Percentage lost of all games played	72*
Percentage of finals lost	100*
Worst flag drought	9 yrs, 1987-95
Current flag drough	9 yrs

Longest losing sequence	12, 1990-91
Lowest score	2.5 v Hawthorn, 1988
Wooden spoons	2 1990, 1991

OTHER SHAMEFUL EFFORTS

ON FIELD: Geelong's 37.17 kicked against Brisbane in 1992 is that club's record score.

OFF FIELD: The coaching appointments and sackings in the early years were harder to fathom than an Arts Festival play. Peter Knights was sacked halfway through his third term in 1989. His replacement, Paul Feltham, had some reasonable on-field success before he was sacked prior to 1990 and replaced by Norm Dare, who lasted just one year before Robert Walls arrived and slowly built the club towards the finals.

On-field success was made more difficult by the original decision to locate the Bears at Carrara instead of Brisbane. As with Sydney, the experiment of private ownership of a football club was a flop. Neither the Bears nor the Victorian clubs, who so shamefully filled their pockets with licence fees, benefited from a weak Brisbane.

A move to the Gabba, an egalitarian club and greater understanding of the need for strong interstate clubs by Victorian-based clubs resulting in various concessions, have all advanced the Bears to a point where Fame may be about to run Shame out of town.

DOOM RECRUITS

'WENT TO BUY A FULL-FORWARD BUT WERE SOLD THE DUMMY'

Even allowing for the handicap under which they started, Brisbane made some dud recruiting decisions. Instead of recruiting players who could get the ball, they went for glamour full-forwards.

Brisbane paid Warwick Capper enough spondulicks that the lank-haired one could fix himself up with tight shorts and thongs for the rest of his life. Capper managed 71 goals in 34 games (1988-90). Not too bad in a weak team that won't pass you the pill. The brains trust decided that they better get another goal sneak on board, so in came South Australian Laurie Schache (1991-2) managing 64 goals in 29 games. Somebody decided he was a bit slow so next they snared the number 1 draft pick of '92, Claremont's John Hutton. He had a couple of bags of 8 and not much else (18 games, 43 goals).

These three players might not have done much but even Peter Hudson would have been struggling with the service from up-field.

Below are two teams selected from Brisbane recruits. In UPPER case is a team comprised of WA and SA recruits. In lower case a team from the rest. Beneath each player's name in brackets are the years the player played for the Bears, where the player came from and how many games he played for the Bears.

With hot-air from the owners mixing with the cold blast coming from the fast revolving clubroom door, it's no wonder that part of the world is prone to cyclones.

Lower case kicking down:

Allan Giffard	Jamie Duursma	Adam Kerinaiua
(1987, 1 game)	(1987, Syd, 1)	(1992, 3 games)
LAURIE SCHACHE	JOHN HUTTON	MATT RENDELL
(1991, Torrens, 29)	(1992, Cl, 19)	(1992, Torr-Fitz, 13)
Robert Mace	Russell Jeffrey	Neil Gaghan
(1988, St K, 1)	(1992, St K, 8)	(1987, Car, 3)
KEN JUDGE	JOHN KLUG	SHANE STREMPEL
(1987-8, EF, 17)	(1993, Adel, 0)	(1989-90, SD, 3)
Gavin Keane	Rod McPherson	Heath Shephard
(1990, Ess, 7)	(1987, Foot, 7)	(1992, Coll, 4)
PETER DAVIDSON	B. RETZLAFF	PETER WORSFOLD
(1990, WCE, 7)	(1992, WCE, 15)	(1991-3, SF, 31)

David Cameron
(1991, Gee, 16
KEVIN CATON
(1990, WCE-Fitz, 8)

Rod Owen
(1992, St K-Mel, 9)
DAVID OGG
(1991, SD, 9)

Mark Buckley
(1987, St K, 4)
STEPHEN WILLIAMS
(1987, PA, 4)

Craig Evans
(1987, Geel, 2)
M. MURPHY
(1993, NM-AD, 10)

Warwick Capper
(1988-90, Syd, 34)
BEN HARRIS
(1987-90, PA, 14)

Matthew Ryan
(1991-2, Col-Syd, 18)
PAUL PEOS
(1993-4, WCE, 33)

RUCKS
Darren Carlson
(1987-90)
Craig Potter
(1991-2, SS, 13)
Gary Shaw
(1987, Coll, 6)

NEIL HEIN
(1987-8, Nor, 15)
ADAM GARTON
(1987-8, Glen, 3)
BRAD ROWE
(1990-1, EF, 14)

Those who miss out:
Peter Curran (1991-2, Haw, 14)
Frank Dunnell (1987-8, Ess, 15)
Troy Lehman (1993-4, Coll, 13)
Peter Smith (1987, NM, 4)
Paul Spargo (1993, NM, 9)

CARLTON

The greatest shame associated with the Blues comes from flagrant fisticuffs such as the 1910 and 1945 Grand Finals (*see DOG DAY AFTERNOONS*). Other than that, and the 'Bongo' Lang (*see CHEATS*) scandal, the Blues appear fairly shame free. Which is a shame!

Percentage lost of all games played 37
Percentage lost of Grand Finals   43
Percentage lost of all finals   50
Worst flag drought   22 yrs, 1916-37
Current flag drought   0
Longest losing sequence   14, 1901-02
Lowest score   0.06 v Coll, 1898
Wooden spoon   0
Worst placing   7th, 1897-1901,
                                   11th, 1991

ONE THAT GOT AWAY

No club specialises in letting talent go like Carlton. Maybe they reckon they have too much as it is? Here are some classic Carlton bungles going way back.

Edward Baker played 1 game (1920) before making a great career at Collingwood and Geelong. He captained Geelong's 1931 premiership side. Chris Bond played 22 games (1990-92) before being dumped. At Richmond he has established himself as one of the best taggers in the game. Gordon Casey (1968) after 1 game went to Footscray (125 games). Frank Coghlan overlooked by the Blues played 109 games with the Saints. Harry Curtis criticised and dumped after a couple of games (1913) went on to play 122 games and kick 149 goals with Collingwood. Glen Denning (1935-7), after 18 Blues' games crossed to Fitzroy where he played 159 games and won a State guernsey. George Dougherty (1934-6). After 17 Carlton games he went to Geelong for 121 games, 191 goals and a flag.

Douglas Nicholls (1932-7). Trained with Carlton but left because of racial slurs. He played 54 games with Fitzroy and won State selection. Denis Pagan dumped without being given a senior game played 120 games for North Melbourne (1967-74) and 23 with South Melbourne (1975-6). He also represented Victoria. Ted Pool came from Kalgoorlie at Carlton's invitation, but when nobody met him at the station he went to Hawthorn (1926-38) for 200 games. He played for Victoria 7 times. Harold Rumney (1925-6) followed 15 games at Carlton with 171 games and a Best and Fairest at Collingwood. He played in 5 premiership sides for the Pies in the backline.

Another lost to Collingwood was Harry Sullivan. After just 31 games (1950-4) he played from 1955-60 at Victoria Park, winning State selection and appearing in a premiership team.

Greg Williams is the one that got away that Carlton got back. Rejected by Carlton he went to Geelong and won a Best and Fairest. Then he left them for the harbour city, becoming a star of the Sydney Swans, winning the Brownlow and guiding them into the finals. In the end Carlton did get him back and he has not let them down.

DOOM RECRUITS

Carlton are often thought of as being the sort of club who buys success. Sometimes things haven't worked out so well for the Blues. Look at these high-profile recruits who went Dark at the Park.

Alex Ruscuklic (1974) 9 games after 109 with Fitz.

Peter Bedford (1977) 5 times Swans' Best and Fairest winner, played just 8 games with the Blues at the end of his career.

Peter McKenna (1977) 11 games after 180 with the Pies.

David Clarke (1982) 9 games after 202 games 298 goals with Geelong.

INTERSTATE RECRUITS WHO NEVER SOARED

Rhett Bayens (1985-6 Perth), Steve Da Rui (East Perth), Brad Shine (1985-88, Swan Districts), Bert Thornley (1968-70, East Fremantle).

COLLINGWOOD

Collingwood have the best winning percentage of all the clubs — no thanks to their efforts in the finals. Having lost over 60% of their Grand Finals the Pies have well and truly earned the catchcry of 'Colliwobbles'. Not only do they tend to lose finals, they also do it in pitiful fashion (*see OTHER SHAMEFUL EFFORTS below*). Only the Crows' fans get close to out-yobbing the Victoria Park gang but when it's all boiled down and said and done, it would be the greatest shame of all if there was no Collingwood.

Percentage lost of all games played 36.2
Percentage of all finals lost   56
Percentage of Grand Finals lost   61
Worst flag drought   31 yrs, 1959-89
Current flag drought   5 yrs
Longest losing sequence   9, 1982
Lowest score   0.08 v South Mel, 1897
Wooden spoons   1: 1976

OTHER SHAMEFUL EFFORTS

Nobody else has managed to equal the Pies' record-losing streak — 8 losses 0 wins — in Grand Finals (1959-89).

The lowest scores in a Grand Final (2.2 v Melbourne, 1960), Second Semi-Final (4.9 v Mel 11.12, 1958) and what use to be the Preliminary Final (5.11 v Essendon 28.6, 1984). The last effort is also the greatest losing margin (133 points) for a Preliminary Final (since 1994 there have been two 'preliminary' finals played — Richmond's 1995 effort of 6.4 outdid the Pies 5.11).

TRADES: Geoff Raines from Richmond (*see ALL TIME WORST TRADES*).

ONE THAT GOT AWAY

The biggest slip-up the Pies ever made was in telling Ted Whitten to come back when he'd filled out. There can't be much doubt that had Whitten played for Collingwood their premiership tally would have been greatly enhanced.

When Bernie Quinlan quit Footscray in 1978, Collingwood were the front-runners to gain his services, but Fitzroy got the signature and again flags went begging.

In 1904 both Alan Belcher and Percy Ogden, who had played just 4 games for the Black and Whites, crossed to Essendon. Alan Belcher notched 176 games, many as captain. Percy Ogden played 161 games for the Dons, captained them in 1919 and captain-coached in 1920-21. He played for Victoria 8 times.

Wally Johnson (1907-16) couldn't get a game in the star-studded Pies but went to Fitzroy for 191 games and played in flag sides and at interstate carnivals.

Tich Utting (1919-22) followed 16 Pies' games with 101 for Hawthorn. Keith Stackpole (1935-9) found there were too many rovers at Collingwood, went to the Roys and in 85 games scored 203 goals. When Harvey Stevens was dumped in 1952 he went to Footscray, won a Best and Fairest and rucked in a flag side.

Doug Searl (1966-8, 12 games) was another to burn at Fitzroy with 131 games and 170 goals.

Ian Bremner played one game before being dumped, went to Hawthorn and played 164 games including 1971 and 1976 flag sides.

Never let it be said that Victoria Park does not appreciate veterans. The Pies have often extended the hand of friendship to a player in the twilight of his career. Usually the on-field results have been less than devastating and one wonders if a youth policy had been pursued the Pies would have claimed a few more flags. Some of those who could not re-ignite their career in a Pies' jersey have been: Ron Andrews, Graeme Atkins, George Bisset, Peter Bradbury, Dermot Brereton, Allan Davis, Tony Elshaug, Warwick Irwin, Ian Low, Barry Mitchell, Paul Morwood, Fraser Murphy, Laurie Sandilands, Graham Teasdale and Michael Woolnough.

Interstaters who died with the Pies include:

Mark Bayliss (South Fremantle, 1989), recruited as a full-forward Bayliss played 4 games and kicked just 6 goals.

Peter Eakins (Subiaco 1970-2, 32 games). An all-Australian Eakins played in the losing 1970 Grand Final side.

Grant Fielke (1987, 16 games, from West Adelaide) never became the dominant player the Pies hoped.

John Parkinson (1971, 3 games, from Claremont) was a Sandover Medallist who suffered from injury and returned home.

Kym Russell (1991) did not manage the success of his brother Scott.

Gary Shaw (1983-6, 32 games, from Claremont) was an expensive buy who never fired a shot.

Bill Valli (1979, 17 games, from West Perth) was another rover, who moved on to Essendon after short service.

Mark Weideman (1981-4, 28 games, from West Adelaide) was never expected to be as good as his father but still proved disappointing.

Murray Wrenstead (1989, from West Coast Eagles) managed just 10 league games, one less than Brett Yorgey (1987, 11 games, from Perth).

At 15 years 287 days old Keith Bromage (1953-6) was the youngest player to play VFL footy. He played 28 games before going to Fitzroy.

ESSENDON

Not much shame to talk of here. The Bombers win often and their flags are pretty regular.

Percentage lost of all games played	41
Finals percentage lost	44
Grand Final percentage lost	48
Worst flag drought	18 yrs, 1966-83
Current flag drought	2 yrs
Longest losing sequence	14, 1933-47
Lowest score	0.09 v Fitz, 1899
Wooden spoons	3: 1907, 1921, 1933

OTHER SHAMEFUL EFFORTS

WEAK AGAINST THE WEAK
Essendon seem to reserve their worst efforts for the least successful clubs.

The Sydney Swans/South Melbourne kicked their highest score 36.20 (1987) against the Bombers, while St Kilda (1973) kicked a record Elimination Final score of 24.14 to Essendon's 13.13.

Most of the Bombers' lowest scores against other clubs go way back to the turn of the century, but 2.11, their lowest against Footscray, was kicked in 1955. Their First Semi-Final 5.11 v Footscray in 1953 is a record low for any team.

ONE THAT GOT AWAY

What is it that the Bombers have against tall blokes?

John Barnes played just 12 games between 1987-90, went to Geelong and has established himself as their finest ruckman in many years.

But that's nothing compared to 'Harry'. Big Justin Madden notched 45 games before moving to Carlton. Now, with over 300 games, 2 Best and Fairests, 2 flags and numerous Brownlow votes, Madden has stamped himself as an all-time great.

At least with Madden the match committee had an excuse — Justin wanted to head to Carlton because brother Simon was restricting his opportunities. But back in 1922 there was no such excuse with Jack Moriarty. Moriarty played 13 games and headed the Dons' goal kicking in his only full year. Dropped for the Preliminary Final and confined to the 2s for a year, he crossed to Fitzroy and immediately clicked. In 1924 he kicked 82 goals to top the goal kicking with the highest tally to that time. In 1927 he bettered that by 1, and in 1928 kicked 12 goals in a game against North. All-up for Fitzroy he played 157 games and kicked 626 goals.

Other slip-ups: Jack O'Halloran (1950-1, 10 games) played 75 with North Melbourne and another 17 for Footscray. He won North's Best and Fairest in 1953.

Bruce Sloss (1907-8, 3 games) went to South Melbourne (1910-14) for 81 games. Sloss played for Victoria 5 times.

Paul Sproule gave good service to the Red and Blacks (60 games) before he was cleared to Richmond in 1972. There he played 86 games and was a member of the 1973-74 flag sides.

Les Woodfield (1921-2) went to South for 76 games

DOOM RECRUITS

In recent times Essendon have led the way in recruiting. Michael Long, James Hird, Che Cockatoo-Collins have all starred. While things haven't always been so rosy, Essendon has had a much better recruit strike rate than most.

Some high-profile interstate recruits who did struggle at Windy Hill include:

Anthony Antrobus. He won the 1983 Magarey Medal with North Adelaide, but played just 22 games (1987-90) before being shuffled off to St Kilda.

Other South Australians who didn't Thrill the Hill were Brenton Phillips and Andrew Rogers. Phillips came from North Adelaide in 1986 and managed just 10 games before being 'given' to Brisbane. Rogers managed 8 games before moving to Geelong.

Sandgroper duds include Barry Day, Shane Ellis and Willie Dick. The latter two were spec drafts, but Day, recruited in 1979 from West Perth, had a huge reputation he never lived up to, managing a meagre 15 games.

Duds drafted from other VFL/AFL clubs include Brian Brown (1982, Fitzroy), Doug Cox (1984, St Kilda), John Fidge (1991, Brisbane), Michael O'Sullivan (1988, Melbourne), Bill Valli (1980, Collingwood), Geoff Raines (1986, Collingwood), Stephen Pirrie (1985, St Kilda).

Roy Ramsay (1982) came from North Melbourne, played 3 games for the Bombers, and went back to Arden Street. Bernie Jones (1978) was the same story, but he went back to Hawthorn.

After 110 games with Footscray, Ian Morrison (1981) played just 3 games for Essendon, echoing G V Pleass (1904, 4 games with Essendon after 109 with South Melbourne). Arch Snell (1908) played a solitary game at Windy Hill after 92 with Carlton.

Dennis Scanlon (1976-81), recruited from North Hobart was not the superstar predicted, but did manage 66 games.

Fitzroy was a great club. Now they're on the verge of extinction. They last hauled up the premiership flag while McArthur dictated surrender terms to the Japanese. Holden hadn't even run its first car off the production line.

Even before Fitzroy abandoned their Brunswick ground, they were 'spooning' along on the bottom. A switch to the Junction Oval and some new stars saw them play some of the most exhilarating and attractive footy of recent times, but as they wander in the desert of flaglessness their supporter base dwindles. For the Roys, the future has the all the vividness of a Moscow tenement.

Percentage lost of all games played	54
Percentage of all finals lost	42
Percentage of Grand Finals lost	38
Worst flag drought	51 yrs, 1945-95
Current flag drought	51 yrs
Longest losing sequence	27, 1963-65
Lowest score	1.0 v Foots, 1953
Wooden spoons	7: 1916, 1936, 1963, 1964, 1966, 1980, 1995
0 wins in season	1964
1 win in a season	1963, 1966

OTHER SHAMEFUL EFFORTS

THE UN-SENSATIONAL SIXTIES: Fitzroy finished in the bottom three clubs every year between 1962 and 1969 inclusive. Between 1962 and 1979 Fitzroy finished no higher than sixth. And since the start of the 90s they have finished no higher than tenth.

Hawthorn's record score 36.15 (1991) was also kicked against the Roys.

ONES THAT GOT AWAY — A LION SPECIALTY

Who says money isn't everything? A bit more of the folding stuff and Fitzroy could have won three or four flags in the last couple of decades. Mind you, not all these players got away because of lack of funds — some just weren't considered good enough to make the grade at Fitzroy. Leaving out Gary Pert and Paul Roos, who gave huge service to the Lions before they left, this is still a pretty awesome combination of players.

FB	Tim Pekin	Rod Carter	Scott McIvor
HB	Ken Hinkley	Peter Foster	Ross Lyon
C	Michael Gale	Terry Wallace	Michael Turner
HF	John Burns	Craig Braddy	Doug Barwick
FF	John Blakey	Alistair Lynch	Richard Osborne
RK	Glen Coleman	Paul Broderick	Bernie Harris

Letting stars get away is nothing new to Fitzroy, it's a tradition.

At the turn of the century Essendon, Melbourne and Collingwood all benefited greatly from the Roys.

Pat Shea got in 13 games in 1904 for the Roys, went to the Western Australian Goldfields and returned with a huge reputation, which he lived up to at Essendon (140 games, 155 goals) being a prime mover in their 1911 and 12 flag wins. He also played for Victoria 4 times.

Mark Shea (1902-4) also crossed to Essendon where he became a top winger, vice-captain and losing flag-side player in his 71 games.

Considered too small for Fitzroy, Hedley Tomkins (1904) played great football for Melbourne, winning State selection before crossing to East Perth. It was a great shame for footy he lost a leg in World War 1. A few years earlier Dan Moriarty had also switched with success to Melbourne, winning State selection.

The classy winger Edward Drohan (1898-1902) played 77 games for the Roys, including the flag side of 1899 and the runners-up of 1900. He went to the Pies from 1903-08, playing a further 96 games. He was in the Collingwood premiership of 1903.

After just 4 games in 1929, Neville Huggins walked out of Fitzroy over a dispute. He starred for North Melbourne from 1931-5, playing 86 games.

DOOM RECRUITS

Not having the funds to spend freely, Fitzroy haven't suffered dashed expectations to the degree of most other clubs, but there are still some disappointments. As in every club, some of these 'doom recruits' are champions who came to their new club for a last shot. The lack of success they experienced in no way can diminish their great careers, but what they did 'before' ain't no help to their new club.

Doom recruits, with clubs recruited from and games played for Fitzroy in brackets.

1975-6 Jeff Clifton: Coll (9); Max George: Swan Districts (8)
1977 Alan Holmes Coll (1)
1980 Len Thompson: South (13); John Rantall: North (6);
Larry Watson: Ess (4)
1981 John Cassin: North (5)

1984 Kevin Taylor: South (1)
1985 Grant Thomas: North (4)
1986 Brendan Ryan: North (1); Murray Browne: Coll (6),
Peter McCormack: Rich (1)
1987 Allan Sidebottom: St K(1); Michael Roberts: Rich (2)
1989 Kevin Caton: WC (9)
1991 David O'Connell WC (21)
1992 Gavin Exell: Geelong (5)
1994 Jeff Hogg: Richmond

UNFULFILLED

In 1967 Fitzroy named Andrew Kula (16 years 46 days) in a
game against Essendon. It was a ploy to protect Kula from
country zoning. Kula never played another league game.

GEELONG

The Cats shame peaked in the '95 Grand Final. Another bad
Grand Final display, the fifth lost Grand Final in their last 5
tries and 4 in 6 years! Other than these lapses Geelong has been
pretty handy.

Percentage lost of all games played	47
Percentage lost of Grand Finals	57
Percentage lost of all finals	57
Worst flag drought	32 yrs, 1964-95
Current flag drought	32 yrs
Longest losing sequence	16, 1941-44
Lowest score	0.8, 1899 v Fitz
Wooden spoons	5: 1908, 1915, 1944, 1957, 1958

OTHER SHAMEFUL EFFORTS

Gary Sidebottom was not a particularly popular player, but even so, Geelong inducted themselves into the Hall Of Shame when their bus forgot to pick him up on the way to a final!

ONE THAT GOT AWAY

These days Geelong don't let too many champs through their fingers. Good recent players they missed include Mario Bortolotto and Dean Rice.

Back at the turn of the century though, Geelong wasn't so good at recruiting. Here are some players they missed:

Charles Parkin (1899) followed his 2 games with 85 at Melbourne.

Gerald Brosnan (1900) was another. Rejected by Geelong and Essendon he went to the Roys and played 131 games with 160 goals, captaining the team and leading the goal kicking.

Told he was too small by Geelong, William Mahoney (1902) played 115 games with Richmond after just 17 with Geelong.

David Ryan (1906) after 3 games went to Collingwood for 99 more.

DOOM RECRUITS

Phil Baker played 9 games with the Cats after coming from North. Baker returned to North and had a major hand in the 1977 Grand Final.

Brett Bailey (1 game, 1990, Melbourne), John Burns (1979, North Melbourne), Stephen Carey (1986, Essendon), Alan Reid (1983, Essendon), Gary Sidebottom (1981, St Kilda), Trevor Spencer (1991, Melbourne), Maurice O'Keefe (1 game, 1980, St Kilda) and Gary Keane (Fitzroy, 1990) all flopped at Kardinia.

Stephen Hooper, Andrew McNish and Leigh Willison were draft choices from the West who failed to shine.

HAWTHORN

Hawthorn began their VFL days like a shot out of a fudge gun.

Three spoons de wood in their first 4 seasons were their only trophies. Gradually though, they pulled through to become the most successful club of the modern era.

Percentage lost of all games played	53
Percentage of all finals lost	37
Percentage lost of Grand Finals	36
Worst flag drought	36 yrs, 1925-60
Current flag drought	4 yrs
Longest losing sequence	27, 1927-9
Lowest score	1.7 v Mel, 1926
Wooden spoons	11: 1925, 1927, 1928, 1932, 1941, 1942, 1946 1949, 1950, 1953, 1965
0 wins in a season	2: 1928, 1950

OTHER SHAMEFUL EFFORTS

For their first 30 seasons Hawthorn managed better than 8th only once (5th in 1943). In each of their first 11 seasons they finished in the last 3.

Carlton's record score 30.30 (1969) was kicked against Hawthorn.

The 'swarm and rush', the deliberate 15-metre penalties, the congested centre bounce were all ugly (though undeniably successful) tactics bred at Glenferrie. Gradually the league has reacted to the decline in spectacle created by such moves and has legislated to outlaw them.

Gary Ablett, one of the few footballers to whom the tag 'genius' can truly be applied, managed just 6 games and 9 goals for the Hawks in 1982. After a short break he started with Geelong and never looked back. To the finals in 1995, Ablett had added 223 games and 939 goals. In Hawthorn's defence, they have won 5 flags since they waved Gary bye-bye, Geelong have won none.

Norman Hillard (1933-37) was no Gary Ablett, but he shared something in common — success after Hawthorn. Hillard only managed 32 games at the Hawks, went to Fitzroy for 94 more, including best-on-ground in the 1944 Grand Final.

Alan Hird (14 games, 1938-9) went to Essendon for 102 games straight. He played on a half-back flank in the 1942 flag side.

A reserves regular who couldn't break through at Hawthorn, Brett Lovett went to Melbourne and had made over 197 league appearances as we went to press. Lovett ran fourth in the 1990 Brownlow and has made numerous State side appearances.

Barry Rowlings (1975-8, 82 games) was traded to Richmond because the Hawks felt a knee injury had finished his career. He played 152 games with the Tigers, winning their Best and Fairest in '79, and captaining them in '83 and '84.

DOOM RECRUITS

The Hawks have been pretty successful with their recruiting but some players who snuck under their guard include:

South Australians Andrew Bennett (1980-4), Robert Day (1971) and Clayton 'Candles' Thompson, and Sandgropers Craig Hoyer (1981-2) and Steve Malaxos (1985).

Andrew Demetriou (3 games, 1988, from North) Vincent Doherty (1940, 5 games) after 96 games with Collingwood, including 2 flags, Roger Ellingworth (1986, 1 game, from Melbourne), Grant Fowler (2 games, 1983-4, from Essendon),

Austin Crabb (1992, 9 games, from Geelong) and Ricky Nixon (8 games, 1992, from St Kilda) were others who were quiet at their new home.

MELBOURNE

The Demons are one of those up-and-down sides. They could open a soup kitchen with their wooden spoons, but they win most of their finals matches. Their current flag drought is the worst in their history and they have signed some high-profile and very dud recruits in their time.

Percentage lost of all games played	52
Percentage of all finals lost	37
Percentage of Grand Finals lost	25
Worst flag drought	31 yrs, 1965-95
Current flag drought	31
Longest losing sequence	20, 1981-82
Lowest score	0.2 v Fitz, 1899
Wooden spoons	9: 1905, 1906, 1919, 1923, 1951, 1969, 1974, 1978, 1981

OTHER SHAMEFUL EFFORTS

Fitzroy's record score 36.22 (1979) and St Kilda's 31.18 (1978) were both kicked against Melbourne, while the Demons also hold the shameful record of worst Grand Final flogging, 96 points. That came in 1988 at the hands of Hawthorn (Haw 22.20 d Mel 6.20).

Only Carlton have given away more good players than the Demons.

Some of the champions the Demons should have had include:

Doug Wade. Wade tried out in practice games, but never made it with the Red and Blues. He played 267 games and kicked 1,058 goals for Geelong and North Melbourne, playing in flag sides for both. He won a Best and Fairest at Geelong.

William Morris (1942-51) managed 141 games for Richmond after 1 reserve game for Melbourne. He played for the state, won a club Best and Fairest and was runner-up in the 1948 Brownlow.

Jim Dorgan (1949, 3 games) went to South for 102 games and won a Best and Fairest.

Pompey Elliott (1899) after 14 games managed 197 with Carlton.

Alan Ezard 180 games, 200 goals with Essendon.

Vin Gardiner (1905), rejected after 2 games, went to Carlton for 157 games and 338 goals. A year earlier, Edward Wade had left after 1 game and gone to South Melbourne. He was part of the 1909 flag side.

Andrew Hislop (1915, 1 game) went to Richmond. In 128 games he was best-on-ground during 2 flag wins.

John Reid's 3 games (1972-4) were followed with a solid 78 for Footscray.

DOOM RECRUITS

Some high-profile recruits who were 'all at sea at the G' include South Australians Jim Tilbrook (1971-75), Graham Molloy (1970-5), and Barry Norseworthy (1977-9). From Western Australia Brian Cook (1977) and Warren Dean (1987-9) drizzled more than sizzled.

Virtually every other Victorian club has sent a high-profile 'doomer' to the Demons — Ken Roberts (Essendon), Phil Carman (Collingwood), Vin Catoggio (Carlton), Philip Egan (Richmond), Rod Owen (St Kilda), Michael Pickering (Richmond), Xavier Tanner (North Melbourne), and Kelvin Templeton (Footscray) never recaptured their early form, or ran into injury woes.

Melbourne even managed an international doomer. Paul Earley (1984) was the original Irish recruit who arrived and left early.

NORTH MELBOURNE

Just like Brisbane in recent times, North Melbourne started off as cannon fodder. The Kangas' last twenty years though has been much better and gradually those bad stats have been stemmed.

Percentage lost of all games played	58
Percentage lost of all finals	56
Percentage lost of Grand Finals	66
Worst flag drought	50 yrs, 1925-74
Current flag drought	18 yrs
Longest losing sequence	35, 1933-35
Lowest score	2.7 v Geelong, 1930
Wooden spoons	13: 1926, 1929, 1930, 1931, 1934, 1935, 1937, 1940, 1956, 1961, 1968, 1970, 1972
0 wins in a season	3: 1926, 1931, 1934

OTHER SHAMEFUL EFFORTS

Melbourne just love playing North Melbourne. North's 1987 effort of 5.10 v Melbourne 22.16, is both the lowest score and greatest thrashing in an Elimination Final. Plus, Melbourne's highest score has been kicked against the Kangas — twice! Melbourne set a Demons' scoring record with 28.14 in 1986, then matched it in 1991.

Adelaide's highest score 28.12 (1991) was also kicked against North.

ONES THAT GOT AWAY

The Kangaroos have managed to let a few champions slip through their paws, including Brownlow Medallists Tony Liberatore and Scott Wynd (both to Footscray) and Brian Wilson (to Melbourne). Dick Clay (213 games at Richmond) was another big loss and Les Parish (87 games with Fitzroy) and Shane Zantuck (1974-6 — after 5 games went to South Melbourne for 56 games and Melbourne for 88 games) could have been useful contributors.

DOOM RECRUITS

Because they have recruited a lot — sometimes with spectacular success, the Roos are also well represented in this category.

Brilliantly performed interstate recruits who were 'nardin at Arden' include: Graham Cornes (1979, 5 games, from Glenelg) Russell Ebert (1979, from Port Adelaide) and Peter Spencer (1981-2, 24 games, from East Perth). Spencer and Ebert both won their State's highest award both before and AFTER their Northern Exposure.

Less high-profile 'doomers' were Mark Brayshaw (Claremont) and Mario Turco. An average player for most of his career, Turco played the best 3 games of his life during the '79 WAFL final series, was recruited to North and played just

9 games. He then resumed his career with East Fremantle.

Barry Pascoe (1967, 15 games) stood out of football for a season to play with the Roos then left after a pay dispute.

From local clubs, North often recruited players who did not repeat their successes at Arden Street. On other occasions the players repeated non-successes at previous clubs. The North's 'gloomers' include:

Thomas Jenkins, (1927, 3 games) after coming from Essendon (1921-25) where he played 65 games and kicked 153 goals.

Arthur Batchelor (1932, 3 games), after 113 with Fitzroy.

Alec Albiston (1950). He played 170 games and scored 383 goals for Hawthorn (1936-49), crossed to North after a dispute and managed 7 games and 6 goals.

John Frazer (1976, 10 games). Adrian Gallagher (1976, 1 game) from Footscray.

Daryl Cumming (1978, 1 game) from Melbourne.

Shane Bond (1979) from Collingwood.

Ian Dunstan (1984, 6 games) after 172 games with Footscray. Grant Thomas (1984, 7 games) from St Kilda.

Rod Lewis (1985, 1 game) from Fitzroy.

Robert Saggers (1986, 3 games) from Sydney.

Michael Murphy (1988, 3 games) and Darren Ogier (1988, 2 games), both from Carlton.

Marty Christensen (1992) from Geelong. Richard Dennis (1992) from Carlton. Glenn Page (1992) from Sydney.

Greg Eppelstun (1993, 1 game) from Footscray. Brendan Bower (1993) from Essendon.

RICHMOND

Richmond are never long without a flag. Richmond are never long without a new coach. No doubt about it, the Tigers have the greatest bent to fratricide in the comp. Not even K-Tel have as many knives as you'll find in the backs of Tigerland personalities. In comparison to the great recruits they've had, Richmond have suffered few 'doomers'. Trouble is, those recruits cost dollars and if on-field success goes missing it's another crawl-on-the-belly year for those left.

Percentage lost of all games played	47
Finals percentage lost	39
Grand Final percentage lost	55
Worst flag drought	23 yrs, 1944-66
Current flag drought	15 yrs, 1981-95
Longest losing sequence	14, 1961-62
Lowest score	0.08 v St K, 1961
Wooden spoons	4: 1917, 1960, 1987, 1989

OTHER SHAMEFUL EFFORTS

Besides being an example of atrocious kicking, the Tigers 2.20 against Hawthorn in 1975 was their lowest score against that club. Other modern day nadirs include 4.8 v Adelaide in 1993 and 2.11 v Footscray in 1958.

The Tigers 6.4 v Geelong 20.9 (1995) was a record low score for a Preliminary Final.

TRADES

Swapped Bill Morris for Galbraith (1944).

Swapped Teasdale, Roberts and Jackson to South for John Pitura (*see ALL-TIME DUD TRADES*).

SHORT PEOPLE

Richmond's Achilles heal appears to be player size: if you're little, you don't get a go in Tigerland. Here are some pretty reasonable players they rejected as too small.

Jack James (1915). James went to St Kilda and played 123 games as one of the best rovers of his time.

Thorold Merrett. Played 180 games for Collingwood and represented Victoria.

Ricky Jackson played 80 games for Melbourne and made the State side.

SHORT STAY

Syd Barker (1908) played 2 games. He later played for Essendon with great success, being captain-coach of the Dons' 1923-4 flag sides.

AND A BET EACH WAY

After 5 games in 1968 Wayne Walsh was traded to South for $500. He played 63 games there before Richmond bought him back for $8,000. It turned out a good deal as Walsh was a fine servant for the club.

DOOM RECRUITS

Collingwood have been very generous giving the Tigers a number of players who weren't in the hunt at the Punt. These include:

Reginald Baker (1928), who played 60 games, including 2 losing Grand Finals before switching to Tigerland for 10. Donald Balfour (1945-6), Ross Brewer (1982-3), Peter

McCormack (1986, 4 games) and Rod Oborne (1979-81, 6 games) also came from the Pies.

In recent times a number of Fitzroy players have helped Richmond. Three who didn't make a difference were Peter Burke (1987), Andrew Cross (1986) and Mark Trewella (1991). The Demons saw David Williams, Steven O'Dwyer and Simon Eishold switch to Richmond without suffering greatly.

Percy Ellin (1910, 1 game, after 70 games with St Kilda), Michael Roberts (1986, 12 games, after 77 at Moorabbin) and Ian Baker (1980) were Saints who didn't move the earth at their new home.

Terry Wallace fired before and after Richmond but not during his stint. Alan Noonan came too late, Richard Murrie, Andrew Underwood and Daryl Sutton didn't work out.

Neither did Craig Balme (1983), Anthony Banik (1990-93) and Dan Foley (1983-5). While Glynn Hewitt (1973-4) and Ray Boyanich were big rep recruits who failed to live up to the hopes held.

ST KILDA

As mentioned in THE WORST OF THE WORST, St Kilda are on their own when it comes to shame. Here are some highlights on the Saints dishonour board.

Percentage lost of all games played	63
Percentage lost of finals	60
Percentage lost of Grand Finals	75
Worst flag drought	69 yrs, 1897-1965 *
Current flag drought	29 yrs
Longest losing sequence	48, 1897-1900

Lowest scores	Pre-WW2 – 0. 1 v Geelong, 1899 Post-WW2 – 4. 8 v Melbourne, 1994 3.18 v W Coast, 1988
Wooden spoons	25*: 1897–1902,1904, 1909, 1910, 1920, 1924, 1943, 1945, 1947, 1948, 1952, 1954, 1955, 1977, 1979, 1983–86, 1988
0 wins in a season	5: 1897, 1898, 1899, 1901, 1902*

The six successive wooden spoons 1897-1902 (inc) is a VFL/AFL record and the four successive 1983-86 (inc) is runner-up to that record. Only Sturt's recent efforts in South Australia better the Saints love of wood, but no other club comes close to the Saints 5 blank slates. Amazingly, on 4 other occasions the Saints have won just a solitary game in the season. Nine seasons for 4 wins! It's doubtful if any major league club anywhere in the world could match that.

One has to admire the Saints' consistency. Not only are they shocking over all games, they carry this through into Grand Finals, and to a lesser degree finals in general.

OTHER SHAMEFUL EFFORTS

Speaking of consistency! St Kilda don't rest on turn-of-the-century laurels. The Saints' recent history shows that not only can they lose lots of games, but they can lose them by big margins. Three clubs have kicked their record score while St Kilda has been the opposition:

CLUBS TO HAVE KICKED THEIR RECORD
SCORE AGAINST ST KILDA

Richmond 34.18, 1980
Footscray 33.15, 1978
Collingwood 32.19, 1980

How (with one notable exception) the Pies love playing the Saints! Not only a record score, but for 43 years St Kilda went without beating Collingwood at Victoria Park. The Saints also went another stretch of 17 years between 1976 and 1993 without winning at the Pies' home ground.

And it's not just Collingwood who love playing the Saints. When they lost to Carlton in round 13 of 1994, St Kilda became the first club in VFL/AFL history to have been beaten 150 times by another club. The margin almost matched the number of Carlton wins — 120 points!

SCARCE GOALS

Boy those early Saints were diabolical: in 1897 A Stewart shared the club's goal kicking award with just 6 majors.

ONES THAT GOT AWAY

Contemporary players who escaped the Saints' doom-laden net include Mick Malthouse, Mick McGuane, Val Perovic, Russell Greene and Ian Stewart (*see ALL-TIME DUD TRADES, for the last two*).

In the Saints' early days, nobody who was any good wanted to stay with them.

After 1 game Jack Purse (1898) went to Melbourne for 109 more and played for Victoria.

James Jackson (1909) was another whose solitary Saints' game marked the start of a great career — at Collingwood, where he went for 93 games and a flag.

Joe Prince (1908-9) played a mere 2 games before being rejected and going to South for 103 more.

William Tymms played 8 games, couldn't make the grade and went to Prahran before trying again at Melbourne with great success: 91 games, a premiership and 5 games in a Victorian jumper.

DOOM RECRUITS

Some people think any fad coming out of New York or Paris must be IT.

The Saints are more entranced by a closer territory: Carlton.

Any Carlton reject has a chance of becoming a Saint. Sometimes it has even paid off for St Kilda: Wow Jones, Peter McConville and Ken Sheldon gave St Kilda good, albeit limited, service. That sort of recruit though has been in the minority.

Former Blues who haven't torn up the Moorabbin turf include: Peter Brown (1981-2, 20 games), Mark Buckley (1985, 7 games), Neil Chandler (1974, 6 games), Peter Fitzpatrick (1980, 4 games), Alex Marcou (1987-8, 24 games), Ian Muller (1988-91, 21), H Pye (1903, 2 games) and Greg Sharp (1984, 6 games).

After Carlton, Essendon, Melbourne and North Melbourne have provided the Saints with fizzer recruits, some high profile.

Melbourne's less-than-helpful-hand-me-downs include Eric Peck (1924) and Hugh Dunbar (1930), while Brian Wilson, Steve Turner and Steven Clarke played 25 games for the Saints combined.

Essendon have contributed Rene Kink (1986), Tom Reynolds (1945) and Brian Winton (1989), while ex-North players were Jim Krakouer, John Reeves (1955) and Colin Thornton (1954).

With games played for the Saints in brackets, interstate hopefuls who imploded rather than exploded include: Ian

Dargie (10), Milan Faletic (24), Daryl Hewitt (26), Greg Jones (2), Gary McDonald (14), Graeme Scott (18).

Leaving out package deals for swaps, the Saints' top draft picks 1986-93 have been Steven Sims (0 games), Michael Quirk (0 games), Jody Arnol (13), Brodie Atkinson (2) and Michael Frost (11).

SYDNEY/ SOUTH MELBOURNE

The Swans have gone in the opposite direction to most clubs: they started at the manor house then regressed to spend 60 years in the pits. When they last won a flag Hitler was still growing his moustache. Since moving to Sydney they have tasted some almost highs and some very low lows.

Percentage lost of all games played	55
Percentage of all finals lost	60
Percentage of Grand Finals lost	73
Worst flag drought	62 yrs, 1934–95*
Current flag drought	62 yrs *
Longest losing sequence	29, 1972–3
Lowest score	0.5 v Carlton, 1899
Wooden spoons	11: 1903, 1922, 1938, 1939, 1962, 1971, 1973, 1975, 1992–4

Clubs to have kicked their highest scores against the Swans are:

Brisbane 33.21, 1993
North Melbourne 35.19, 1993
Fremantle 25.13, 1995

At half-time in the 1993 Brisbane game, the Bears led 19.10 to 0.4. This is the biggest ever half-time lead in the AFL. What makes this thrashing even more SHAMEFUL for the Swans is that the Bears were the second-bottom club!

The 1898-9 South Melbourne team produced some fabulously menial scores. Besides the lowest of 0.5 mentioned above there were: 0.9 v Essendon (1899), 1.2 v Geelong (1898), 1.4 v Fitzroy (1898) and 1.7 v Collingwood (1898).

In recent times, one of Sydney's more remarkable efforts was to score just 3.10 against Richmond in 1984.

It's not just on the playing side where the Swans can be embarrassing — there's their name for a start. Swan? Who's afraid of the big bad Swan? At one time they were the Bloods, but somebody with the literary bent of Brute Barnard obviously decided that alliteration was the way to go. ('Brute Barnard' was not idly picked.)

The Swans played by the lake, there were swans at the lake, so why not the South Melbourne Swans? 'Cause it's a dumb name that's why! Had they moved to Canberra or Tassie they might have been spared the nickname, but the new home was Sydney and in the name of chronically bad alliteration the dreaded 'S' stayed.

We think it's time Sydney became The Push — or Sydney Sin or Plugger's Tugs — anything but the Swans!

(*See WORST PROMOTIONS for a fuller lowdown on Sydney follies.*)

Now we know what happened to the Air New Zealand computer that crashed a plane into Mount Erebus — it got sold to the Swans as a recruiting device!

Yes, it's hard to get uncontracted players up to the Harbour city, yes the draft is a lottery, but have a look at Sydney's top draft choices (excluding special ACT/ NSW region concessions), 1986-93!

SYDNEY'S TOP DRAFT PICKS

John Brinkkotter (1986): 10th overall —5 games.

Michael Parsons (1987): 10th overall — 25 games.

Dion Scott (1988): 8th overall — 6 games.

Brad Tunbridge (1989): 8th overall — 50 games.

W McKenzie (1990): swapped No 2 pick with Carlton (who chose James Cook) — 21 games.

A McGovern (1991): 4th overall.

S Watters and A Begovich (1992): 1st pick swapped with West Coast Eagles.

Darren Gaspar (1993): No 1 priority pick.

Only Tunbridge gave the Swans any substantial service. Scott, McGovern, Gaspar and Watters are pursuing careers at other clubs at the time of writing.

TRADES

All the credit for the John Pitura trade (*see DUD TRADES*) went out the window when the Swans, in one of the all-time bad trades, swapped Terry and Neale Daniher to Essendon in exchange for Neville Fields.

Wayne Carey, John Longmire and James Hird could all be in the Swans colours had the Swans' admin been more on the ball.

While the Swans were obsessed with star players and big salaries though, these youngsters were off establishing themselves as the new stars.

Collingwood have reason to thank the Swans. Darren Millane made it through the Swans net and Shane Morwood (17 games with South Melbourne) played 194 times with the Pies after refusing to make the Sydney move.

The Saints were glad of South Melbourne back in the '20s. Roy Bence (15 games for the Swans in 1922) went to St Kilda and played 144 games. Harold Neill, the Saints' Best and Fairest in 1931, played 2 games in 1925 with South before his distinguished career with St Kilda.

Earlier still, Thomas Clancy's 1 game in red and white was followed by 74 games for the Blues, 1910-14.

William Deans (1941) rejected after 1 game, crossed to Melbourne for 135 games and a flag.

DOOM RECRUITS

Dermott Brereton. Recruited to the Swans in 1994 after establishing himself as one of the all-time greats, Dermott was suspended (8 weeks) for standing on Hawthorn's Raydon Tallis' head before the season proper had even commenced. Later in the year, after indifferent form, he received another 7 week suspension for striking.

Brereton was one of the few big name recruits who haven't succeeded at Sydney. The Red and Whites troubles have been more in establishing new players at their club.

To get an idea of the amount of players that have NOT made a difference to the Swans in the last sixteen seasons, check out the two teams below. They are comprised of Swans recruits 1979-87 and 1988 onwards who offered more gloom than zoom.

SWANS RECRUITS 1979-87 V SWANS RECRUITS 1988–

The 1979-87 SwansS kicking down.

FB Gary Cowton (1981)	N Jenkinson (1980)	P Melesso (1981)
T Malakellis (1993)	John Hutton (1993)	Shane Fell (1990)
HB John Favier (1985)	Bill Picken (1984)	D Henderson (1983)
Darren Ogier (1989)	D Brereton (1994)	Jim West (1990)
C Rudy Yonson (1985)	M Davis (1984)	K Taylor (1981)
Gary Stevens (1992)	Jim Silvestro (1988)	Matt Ryan (1990)
HF Vin Catoggio (1983)	Daryl Sutton (1983)	M Scott (1985)
Aldo Dipetta (1993)	Stuart Wigney (1991)	P Starbuck (1990)
FF Jim Edmond (1986)	M Oaten (1980)	D Stirling (1983)
Tony Begovich (1993)	Tim Barling (1989)	David Wittey (1990)
RK Trevor Mustey (1983)	G Neesham (1982)	Paul Callery (1980)
M Parsons (1988)	Robert Kerr (1990)	A Battiston (1988-9)

INTERCHANGE

John Lucas (1982-4)	Peter Caven (1995)
Robert Prosser (1985)	Paul Holdsworth (1989)
Peter Quirk (1987)	John Brinkkotter (1988-89)
John Reid (1982-3)	Michael Lockman (1988)
Robert Saggers (1985)	Allan Mckellar (1992)
Jamie Siddons (1984)	Robert Neil (1992)
Anthony Sinclair (1985)	Darren Gaspar (1994-5)
Andrew Pud Smith (1985)	Chris O'Dwyer (1990-1)
Tony Smith (1986-8)	Michael Phyland (1987-90)
Lindsay Sneddon (1985)	Dion Scott (1990 and 1992)
Daryl Vernon (1983-4)	Brian Stanislaus (1991)
Mark Whitzell (1981-6)	David Strooper (1992-3)
David Winbanks (1981-3)	Robert Teal (1989-90)
Len Thompson (1979)	Andrew Thompson (1993)
Daryl Cumming (1979)	Alan Thorpe (1992)
Robert Lamb (1979)	Michael Werner (1993)

The amazing statistic is that between them Rod Carter, Mark Bayes and Stevie Wright played more games for the Swans than all the above players combined!

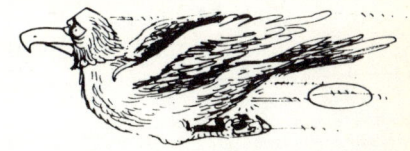

WEST COAST EAGLES

The Eagles have regrettably been relatively idiot proof since their inception. There was some palaver talked about their guernsey design at the time — how the 'eagle' faced east and was going to savage the Victorian teams — but interestingly that has faded as the colours have darkened. Some of the players have been involved in appalling adverts too, but on field embarrassment has been minimal.

Percentage lost of all games played	37
Percentage of all finals lost	28
Percentage of Grand Finals lost	33
Worst flag drought	4 yrs, 1988-91
Current flag drought	1 yr
Longest losing sequence	6, 1989
Lowest score	1.12 v Essendon, 1989

OTHER SHAMEFUL EFFORTS

While the Eagles' First Qualifying score (1995) of 8.7 is a record low, most of the Eagles' shame relates to their bad patch in 1989.

Around the time of the Essendon fiasco, John Todd trained the Eagles so hard Paul Peos collapsed through fatigue.

As if things couldn't get worse for the Eagles after the Essendon thrashing, runner Brian Douge knocked himself unconscious when he ran into the elbow of skipper Murray Rance.

Douge must have been severely concussed because a day later he called for the development of a muddy ground in Perth

241

to help prepare for Victorian conditions.

Mick Malthouse subsequently showed that attitude not latitude was the key to playing well in the wet.

ONES THAT GOT AWAY

Darren Bennett, given just 4 games by the Eagles, kicked 215 goals for Melbourne in 74 games, went to the USA and made the 1995 All-Star American Football League team and the Team of Champions. He was also a reserve for San Diego in the 1994 Superbowl.

In 1995 Matt Clape (Carlton) and Matt Connell (Adelaide), both traded by the Eagles, had sensational years at their new clubs.

DOOM RECRUITS

Shane Porter, Darren Bartsch, Brendad Retzlaff, Glenn O'Loughlin, Trent Nichols, Corey Young, Paul Mifka, Sean King, Brent Hutton, Shane Cable, Peter Higgins, Mark Williams, Peter Freeman, Gavin Cooney, Richard Geary.

WAFL CLUB LOWLIGHTS

CLAREMONT

Claremont's supporters would arrive at the outer of other clubs, erect their deckchairs and then complain when other fans stood in front. Prior to the 1980s Claremont were cream-puff, card-carrying nancy boys, but that has all changed and nowadays Claremont are rarely seen down the puce end of town.

Percentage lost of all games played	54
Percentage of all finals lost	43
Percentage of Grand Finals lost	50
Worst flag drought	23 yrs, 1941–63
Current flag drought	2 yrs
Longest losing sequence	18, 1957–58
Lowest score	1.3 v Perth, 1945
Wooden spoons	12

OTHER SHAMEFUL EFFORTS

In round 13, 1995, Claremont kicked a woeful 1.7 (13) to West Perth's 11.18 (74) at Joondalup. This was not quite the Tigers' worst effort but it was in the vicinity.

Leaving aside the underage competition during World War 2, East Perth's highest score of 32.19 was kicked against Claremont in 1958. Bill Mose scored 13 goals for the Royals.

Claremont won only 1 game in each of season's 1926 and 1927.

East Fremantle's George Doig score a club record 19 goals against Claremont in 1934.

(See HQ — POQs for a rundown on the shortfalls of Claremont Oval during the 1940s and 1950s.)

TRADES

Mark Bairstow, Sandover medallist and later Geelong champ and captain, traded to South Fremantle for Bruce Monteath, who was at the end of his career and played only a handful of games for the Tigers.

DOOM RECRUITS

Throughout the 1970s, Claremont embarked on a voracious Victorian recruiting drive. VERDUN HOWELL came over as coach and though he did better than PETER PIANTO before him, the best he managed was runner-up, even with recruits like PETER HINES, DARRYL GRIFITHS, JOHN EVANS, ROBIN GREENWOOD, GEOFF BLETHYN and COLIN TULLY. JOHN MANZIE and BARRY PRICE were two more high-profile recruits who came later. None of the players matched their Victorian reputations, but none were dire either. What did happen was Claremont's junior development was stalled. When that got into gear the Tigers roared.

ALTERNATE ICONS

Players to keep the outer entertained whether by dint of being Skill Impaired, Integrity Challenged, One Stud Short Of A Full Boot, Desperate But Kickless or simply Different include: DALTON GOODING, SIMON LILL, BILL BYRON, DAVID O'CONNELL and MICK MOYLAN.

ALLEN 'SHORTY' DANIELS.

EAST FREMANTLE

Not a lot of shame here, though East do tend to be well represented in the WAFL's all-time high tribunal visitors.

Percentage lost of all games played	38
Percentage of all finals loss	36
Percentage of Grand Finals lost	48
Worst flag drought	10 yrs, 1947–56
Current flag drought	1 yr, 1995
Longest losing sequence	13, 1968, 1970
Lowest score	1.2 v West Perth, 1898
Wooden spoons	1

OTHER SHAMEFUL EFFORTS

In their first season in the competition 1898, East managed only one win.

West Perth's 37.17 (1981) scored against East Fremantle is that club's record score.

The 1977 Grand Final was a shocker for East. Their injury-depleted side had a record score of 26.13 scored against them by Perth.

ONES THAT GOT AWAY

The great Barry Cable wanted to play for East Fremantle, but was told he was too small to get a kick with the big boys.

When East and South Fremantle shared Fremantle Oval, Steve Marsh wandered down to try out for East but bumped into South's players first, trained with them and wound up being one of South's and Western Australia's all-time greats.

Gerard Neesham was let go by East to Swans, where he was instrumental in creating a premiership power. Graham Melrose won a Sandover Medal with East, but like Neesham went to Swans on his return from the east and continued to be a great player.

DUD TRADES

Tony Casserly to Central Districts for Ric Vidovic.

DOOM RECRUITS

Mark Norsworthy, Neville Fields, Ken Newlands and many more.

ALTERNATE ICONS

Players to keep the outer entertained whether by dint of being Skill Impaired, Integrity Challenged, One Stud Short Of A Full Boot, Desperate But Kickless, or simply Different include: ROBERT ZUPANOVIC, BRIAN NEEDLE, SIMON MOSS, JOE PITTORINI, DAVID SPRY, MICK JEZ, PHIL CLUCAS.

PLAYER MOST HATED BY OTHER CLUBS SUPPORTERS

RAY 'TRIZZIE' LAWRENCE.

EAST PERTH

East Perth were one of the powers until the 1980s. Since then they've crawled rather than walked tall, but they still have a way to go before the Hall Of Shame can welcome them with open arms.

Percentage lost of all games played	45
Percentage of all finals lost	48
Percentage of Grand Finals lost	48
Worst flag drought	17 yrs, 1979–95
Current flag drought	17 yrs
Longest losing sequence	15, 1929
Lowest score	0.6 v East Ftle, 1909
Wooden spoons	6

OTHER SHAMEFUL EFFORTS

1 win in a season: 1906.

NEXT BIG THING

GRANT CAMPBELL was always going to be the NBT but though he played over 200 games for the Royals, he never seemed to move much above serviceable. Wearing what looked like a pizza on each knee, Campbell would vainly, yet unflaggingly, chase the ball over the boundary line 30 to 40 times a game.

Players to keep the outer entertained whether by dint of being Skill Impaired, Integrity Challenged, One Stud Short Of A Full Boot, Desperate But Kickless, or simply Different include: TERRY FREEMANTLE, EDDIE PITTER, ARCHIE DUDA.

PLAYER MOST HATED BY OTHER CLUBS SUPPORTERS

JOHN SCOTT.

PERTH

Perth don't have a prayer of challenging Swans or Subiaco for Shame, but long flag droughts and a good clutch of wooden spoons help.

Percentage lost of all games played	52
Percentage of all finals lost	52
Percentage of Grand Finals lost	59
Worst flag drought	47 yrs, 1908–54
Current flag drought	18 yrs, 1978–95
Longest losing sequence	12, 1922–23
Lowest score	0.1 v West Perth, 1899
Wooden spoons	13

The Demons have shame like Bombay has people. Consider these embarrassing entries: in season 1923 they managed a solitary win. They also went 21 games without a win, but managed to draw one and escape that stat as a 'losing sequence'.

Claremont, 39.20, kicked their record score against Perth (1981).

The hopeless Subiaco also kicked their record score 32.12 against Perth (1984). Subiaco like playing Perth. Their First Semi-Final score of 26.13 against Perth, back in 1959, is a record. In that game Subiaco kicked 16 goals to 1 behind in the third quarter (*see FINALS FADEOUTS*).

Perth's flagless streaks are the second and eighth longest in the WAFL's history and their first flag came from a protest based on shakier ground than the San Andreas fault.

ALTERNATE ICONS

Players to keep the outer entertained whether by dint of being Skill Impaired, Integrity Challenged, One Stud Short Of A Full Boot, Desperate But Kickless, or simply Different include: MICK REA, MURRAY COUPER, PETER BOSUSTOW, DEAN HERBERT, GAVIN WHITTINGTON, LEN GANDINI, TODD JENKINS.

PLAYER MOST HATED BY OTHER CLUBS SUPPORTERS

MAL ATWELL.

South are either very good or very bad. They've had a number of flag droughts, they tend to lose Grand Finals and in their early days they couldn't score a goal to save themselves.

Percentage lost of all games played 48
Percentage of all finals lost 50
Percentage of Grand Finals lost 56
Worst flag drought 29 yrs, 1918–46
Current flag drought 15 yrs, 1981–95
Longest losing sequence 12, 1936–37
Lowest score 0.4 v East Ftle, 1904
Wooden spoons 11

OTHER SHAMEFUL EFFORTS

Just 1 win in season 1904.

Perth's highest total, 30.18, scored against South in 1977.

South appear 4 times on our longest premiership drought list. The flagless periods are 1918-46, 1900-15, 1955-69 and 1981-95.

In the wartime underage competition of 1944 South had the greatest losing margin ever recorded: 256 pts v East Perth.

ALTERNATE ICONS

Players to keep the outer entertained whether by dint of being Skill Impaired, Integrity Challenged, One Stud Short Of A Full

Boot, Desperate But Kickless, or simply Different include: 'TURKEY' TOM GRLJUSICH, BOB CARSON, GORDON GATTI, SIMON OUTHWAITE, MARK JACKSON.

PLAYER MOST HATED BY OTHER CLUBS SUPPORTERS

RAY BAUSKIS.

SUBIACO

WORST OF THE WORST has a rundown on Subiaco's less impressive efforts. Unquestionably the most consistent dud club in the WAFL, Subiaco have survived expulsion motions and bankruptcy and now sniff a blossoming future.

Percentage lost of all games played	58
Percentage of all finals lost	57
Percentage of Grand Finals lost	59
Worst flag drought	48 yrs, 1924–72
Current flag drought	8 yrs
Longest losing sequence	29, 1901–3
Lowest score	0.0 v Sth Ftle, 1906*
Wooden spoons	19
0 wins in a season	2: 1902, 1905

OTHER SHAMEFUL EFFORTS

Subiaco managed 1 win only in seasons 1903 and 1982.
Swan Districts kicked a record score of 40.11 against

Subiaco on 11 August, 1979.

Bernie Naylor's 23 goals in a single game, kicked against the Maroons in 1953, is a WAFL record.

Subiaco are one of only two clubs to have gone from premiers to wooden spooners in a season: 1915-16.

(*See CRUD DUDS for an account of the Lions Canary guernsey design.*)

DOOM RECRUITS

See DUDS FROM EAST TO WEST for interstate doomers. Local gloomers include Archie Duda, Bob Johnson, Peter Spencer, Neil Robinson and many more.

ALTERNATE ICONS

Players to keep the outer entertained whether by dint of being Skill Impaired, Integrity Challenged, One Stud Short Of A Full Boot, Desperate But Kickless, or simply Different include: MITCH FUSSELL, BRENDAN McFAULL, GARY FATHERS, JEFF MURRAY, FRANK BUCKNALL.

PLAYER MOST HATED BY OTHER CLUBS SUPPORTERS

LAURIE KEENE.

SWAN DISTRICTS

The Black and Whites suffered from being the last club admitted to the WAFL. They have an impressive collection of wooden spoons, an impressive winless sequence and two solitary-win seasons as credentials for Hall Of Shame nominations. In fact only Subiaco can claim to get near the sordid swag of the Swans.

Percentage lost of all games played	60
Percentage of all finals lost	51
Percentage of Grand Finals lost	30
Worst flag drought	27 yrs, 1934–60
Current flag drought	5 yrs
Longest losing sequence	20
Lowest score	2.8 v East Perth, 1968
Wooden spoons	17

OTHER SHAMEFUL EFFORTS

Swans have not gone through a season without a win but came as close as you can in 1968, when they won only one game, and that by a solitary point when Bill Holmes kicked a long goal after the final siren. Swans also scored only 1 win in 1951.

Claremont's George Moloney's 19 goals against Swans in 1940 is a club record, as is West Perth's Ted Tyson's 17 majors scored against Swans in 1938.

When Gary Sidebottom was coming off the worse in a clash with Stan Magro, members of the Sidebottom family jumped the fence to get involved. This surely ranks as one of the most pants-down stupid episodes in the history of footy.

Swans' fans also earn SHAME points for the time they invaded the oval at half-time and stomped the soil in an effort to destroy the lost contact lens of East Fremantle's Barry Biffin.

NEXT BIG THING

Laurie Andrew and Rod Brown were two teenagers who were supposed to be the champions. Neither reached great heights, but Brown played many solid games for Subiaco.

DOOM RECRUITS

Daryl Sutton, Peter May, Stuart Magee, Ian Cooper and many, many more.

ALTERNATE ICONS

Players to keep the outer entertained whether by dint of being Skill Impaired, Integrity Challenged, One Stud Short Of A Full Boot, Desperate But Kickless or simply Different include: GREG LATHAM, EDDY FLEAY, VLADA RAKICH.

PLAYER MOST HATED BY OTHER CLUBS SUPPORTERS

GARY SIDEBOTTOM.

WEST PERTH

West Perth's history shows successful streaks juxtaposed against troughs of failure. Long winless breaks, premiership droughts and a wooden spoon stretch, 1990–2, are some of the dark side of West Perth's history.

Percentage lost of all games played	44
Percentage of all finals lost	55
Percentage of Grand Finals lost	46
Worst flag drought	26 yrs, 1906–31
Current flag drought	0
Longest losing sequence	27, 1938–9
Lowest score	0.3 v Perth, 1912
Wooden spoons	10

OTHER SHAMEFUL EFFORTS

In season 1939 West Perth managed only 1 win.

South Fremantle's 40.18 (1981) against West is the highest recorded league score in WAFL, aside from the wartime underage games. East Fremantle's 32.23 against West in 1979 is also a record for that club, aside from the under-age competition.

The side went 19 years (1976–94) without a flag, giving it the seventh as well as the fifth longest flagless streak in WAFL history.

NEXT BIG THING

Jeff Hendricks was a champion schoolboy player who began a league career as a teenager and played for many years. In all that time though he rarely rose above the competent and never became the star West had hoped.

ALTERNATE ICONS

Players to keep the outer entertained whether by dint of being Skill Impaired, Integrity Challenged, One Stud Short Of A Full Boot, Desperate But Kickless, or simply Different include: GRAEME COMERFORD, NOEL MUGAVIN, SEAN KING.

PLAYER MOST HATED BY OTHER CLUBS SUPPORTERS

RAY LUCEV.

SANFL CLUB LOWLIGHTS
(FROM 1907)

CENTRAL DISTRICTS

Centrals have never won a flag. They made their first Grand
Final in 1995, 32 years after their entry into the big time.
Centrals do not play well in finals. In fact they are about as
effective as insect repellant on a crocodile, having won just 4
of the 20 finals matches they have contested. After struggling
in their early years of establishment, the Bulldogs these days
seem to win their fair share of games during the season. But
come finals time they're back in the doghouse. They lost 12
finals in a row (1972–94) before their First Semi-final win
over Norwood in '94 by just 4 points. They celebrated while
they could, then were thrashed by Port Adelaide to the tune of
90 points in the Preliminary. Still, wonders never cease, in
1995 they made the Grand Final. Maybe '96 will be their
year?

Percentage lost of all games played	55
Percentage of all finals lost	75
Percentage of Grand Finals lost	100 *
Worst flag drought	32 yrs, 1964–95
Current flag drought	32 yrs
Longest losing sequence	21, 1964–5
Lowest score	1.6 v Port Adel, 1967
Wooden spoons	2

In their relatively short history, Centrals have succeeded in covering themselves in more shame than other clubs have managed in twice the time.

Consider: A record drubbing of 238 points by Glenelg in 1975 (only South Fremantle in the Western Australian wartime underage competition have managed worse) in a game in which Glenelg scored their and SA's highest total of 49.23. In that game Fred Phillis kicked 18 goals, but perhaps the amazing statistic is that there were 31 more he didn't get!

Torrens 137 point thrashing of the Bulldogs in 1964 was that club's biggest victory.

Central 'own' four of the lowest 20 scores in SANFL since 1964: all against Port. Centrals combined total in those 4 shockers is 9.23

GLENELG

In their early days, the bayside club plumbed new depths of ineptitude — 56 losses on the trot and wooden spoons in their first five years established them as something rather special. Then they got it almost all together. They won everywhere but where it counted — on the scoreboard on Grand Final day. Not even Collingwood have a record to match Glenelg's when it comes to Grand Final flutters: just 4 wins in 16 attempts!

Percentage lost of all games played	55
Percentage of all finals lost	46
Percentage of Grand Finals lost	75
Worst flag drought	35 yrs, 1935-72
Current flag drought	10 yrs

Longest losing sequence	56*
Lowest score	2.10 v Torrens, 1926
Wooden spoons	14

OTHER SHAMEFUL EFFORTS

First to last: 1934-35. Yes, Glenelg did the almost impossible, backed up a flag with a wooden spoon.

The second longest flag drought in the SANFL by seasons competed (35 years, 1935–72).

In addition to their groundbreaking run of 56 games without a win (1921–4), they also managed winless streaks of 20 (1935–6) and 16 (1945–6).

NORTH ADELAIDE

North save their shame for Grand Finals. Their 2 lowest scores post-1907 (1.8) have both been scored against Port Adelaide in the premiership decider — 75 years apart.

Percentage lost of all games played	46
Percentage of all finals lost	45
Percentage of Grand Finals lost	52
Worst flag drought	14 yrs, 1932–48
Current flag drought	4
Longest losing sequence	12, 1947–8, 1959
Lowest score	1.8 v Port, 1914 and Port, 1989
Wooden spoons	6

Norwood's highest score of 33.21 was scored against North (1977). It was also the Redlegs GWM (150 pts).

The Eagles kicked a record high 28.20 against North in 1993.

The poor efforts 1989 Grand Final and 1990 finals. (*See FINALS FLUTTERS for details*.)

NORWOOD

The Redlegs aren't a prime candidate for Hall Of Shame status. A big flag drought through the Menzies and Holt years was their worst time.

Percentage lost of all games played	42
Percentage of all finals lost	48 (1907 on)
Percentage of Grand Finals lost	44 (1889 on)
Worst flag drough	24yrs, 1951–74
Current flag drought	7 yrs
Longest losing sequence	11, 1919,1969
Lowest score	0.5 v Port Adel, 1909
Wooden spoons	5

OTHER SHAMEFUL EFFORTS

The lowest score (0.5, 1907) in the SANFL.

A score of just 2.5 in the 1988 Second Semi-Final against Port Adelaide.

PORT ADELAIDE

No shame here except for maybe the Second Semi-Final of
1993. In that game the Eagles held Port to a paltry 4.6 while
scoring 14.20. But that's a rare moment of embarrassment in
Port's history, usually they're the ones inflicting the hiding.

Percentage lost of all games played	29
Percentage of all finals lost	45 (1907 on)
Percentage of Grand Finals lost	46 (1889 on)
Worst flag drought	11, 1965-76
Current flag drought	0
Longest losing sequence	6, 1949-50
Lowest score	1.4 v Norwood, 1909
Wooden spoons	3

SOUTH ADELAIDE

As acknowledged in WORST OF THE WORST, South are
right down there at bedrock. With a whopping 63% of games
lost they are fighting with St Kilda over who should be sleeping
with the giant squids.

Occasionally South rocket to the surface too quick, get the
bends and plummet back down. Neil Kerley's amazing 1964
flag and a sudden improvement in '91 did not herald a fundamental change in the character of South.

Percentage lost of all games played 63 (1907 on)
Percentage of all finals lost   62 (1907 on)
Percentage of Grand Finals lost   54 (1889-95)
Worst flag drought   32 yrs, 1964–95,
                                      1900–1934 (no comp,
                                      1916–18)

Current flag drought   32 yrs
Longest losing sequence   34, 1947–9 (post-1907)
Lowest score   1.4 v Sturt, 1973
Wooden spoons   24

OTHER SHAMEFUL EFFORTS

South Adelaide's flagless streaks are the 4th, 5th and 9th longest in SANFL history.

Clubs to have scored club record totals against South include: North Adelaide 34.22 (1972 — also North's greatest winning margin), Sturt 32.19 (1988) and Torrens 34.15 (1950)

West's 1959 175-point caning of South is the Bloods' biggest win.

South 'own' 5 of the lowest 20 scores in the modern (post-1964) era of the SANFL. This is more than any other club — even Woodville! South's 1.4 against Sturt at Unley in 1973 is THE worst of the modern era.

South own most of the worst losing runs in South Australian footy. In fact 7 of the 12 worst losing streaks including: 34 (1947–9, 2nd worst overall), 26 (1988-89, 3rd worst), 23 (1949–51), 22 (1961–2).

STURT

Sturt were a power during the 1960s and '70s, but the 1990s have proved to be bleaker than a cancer ward. Record high scores and drubbings by former fags, Central Districts and South Adelaide are just some of the humiliating events the old head prefect Sturt has had to wear over the last few years. Port Adelaide's 34.18 (1990) was the highest total ever against Sturt, while Sturt's 2.8 in round 19 last year (1995) against West Adelaide was lower than even the *Hollywood Enquirer* could go. In fact, in a display of awesome ineptitude, in 20 1995 games, Sturt managed to get within 10 goals of the opposition only 5 times — and one of those was by a point!

Percentage lost of all games played	49 (1907 on)
Percentage of all finals lost	49
Percentage of Grand Finals lost	38
Worst flag drought	22, 1941-65 (no comp 1942-44)
Current flag drought	19 yrs, 1977-95
Longest losing sequence	22, 1994-5
Lowest score	2.4 v North Adel, 1920
Wooden spoons	17

OTHER SHAMEFUL EFFORTS

No club comes close to Sturt's 7 consecutive wooden spoons 1989-1995.

The club's current losing streak stands at 22, and Sturt are closing in on South Adelaide as having the second greatest winless streak in SANFL history.

The 1978 Grand Final loss to Norwood was another shameful effort (*see FINALS FADEOUTS*), as were:

A dreadful 3.2 (20) v North Adelaide 27.18 (180) in 1990.

A paltry 2.9 v (21) v Woodville in 1989.

1995 losses of 148 points (v Norwood), 143 points (v Glenelg), 133 points (v Central Districts), 128 points (v West Adelaide).

WEST ADELAIDE

West began life like a lot of other clubs; as shockers. Three times they went through a season without a win. After that burst though they started to put a bit of a gap between themselves and shame, and these days they stand as a middling success story.

Curiously, West have sent more disappointing recruits to the VFL/AFL than any other South Australian club. Mark Weideman, Sefton Parry, Glynn Hewitt, Robert Day, Grant Fielke, Bert Johnson, Jeff Bray, Bruce Lindner and Don Roach all failed to live up to their SA reps.

Percentage lost of all games played	52 (1907 on)
Percentage of all finals lost	43 (1907 on)
Percentage of Grand Finals lost	47 (1889 on)
Worst flag drought	32yrs, 1937–71
Current flag drought	12yrs
Longest losing sequence	17, 1933
Lowest score	1.5 v Port Adel, 1907
Wooden spoons:	13
0 wins in a season:	3: 1898, 1906, 1933

1.7 v Port Adelaide (1908), 2.2 v Port Adelaide (1968), 2.4 v Port Adelaide (1910), 1.10 v North Adelaide (1915), 2.4 v North Adelaide (1920).

The equal third longest flag drought (32 seasons of competition) in the SANFL.

WEST TORRENS

West Torrens of course ceased to exist in their own right back in 1990, merging with Woodville to become Woodville–West Torrens. But that shouldn't prevent us from poking through a woeful record they'd established up to then. West Torrens were one of those sorts of clubs who manage to fall into the finals pretty regularly because the opposition was made up of even worse contenders — South Adelaide, Woodville and so on. They had one of the worst finals records in footy, losing twice as often as they won. West Torrens had two long premiership droughts of 37 (SANFL record) and 27 years.

Percentage lost of all games played 53 (1907 on)
Percentage of all finals lost   65
Percentage of Grand Finals lost   50
Worst flag drought   37 yrs, 1954-90
Longest losing sequence   16, 1976
Lowest score   0.8 v South, 1913
Wooden spoons   5

West Torrens had the 1st and 8th longest flagless streaks prior to their merger with Woodville.

Clubs to score their highest total against West Torrens include West Adelaide 36.21 (1982) and Woodville 29.11 (1982).

West Torrens have been the pants-down record thrashee of clubs Central Districts (margin 198 points, 1988) and Woodville (117 points, 1985).

West Torrens scored 2.9 (1989) and 4.6 (1990) v Norwood. Also, 4.1 v Port in 1965.

WOODVILLE

Sadly now defunct in their own right (having merged with West Torrens, to become Woodville–West Torrens), the Wood-ducks threatened, in their relatively brief history, to dethrone the Saints as the most inept club of all time. In their 27 seasons they never made a Grand Final. In fact, they played in finals in only 3 years of their 27-year reign of ridicule. Their 71% loss record is way above even South Adelaide or St Kilda, and with Brisbane improving in the AFL, chances are it will dominate for many years to come.

All in all, Woodville, during their history as a singular entity, were without doubt the least successful club in the three main comps.

Percentage lost of all games played	71
Percentage of all finals lost	60
Percentage of Grand Finals lost	n a
Worst flag drought	27 yrs, 1964–90

Longest losing sequence	16, 1966–7
Lowest score	2.5 v Port Adel, 1967
Wooden spoons	9

OTHER SHAMEFUL EFFORTS

Clubs to score their highest club total against Woodville include Port Adelaide 37.21 (1980), South Adelaide 39.16 (1984) and Sturt 32.19 (1974). Also, Sturt's greatest winning margin, 162 points, occurred in that match.

Port Adelaide's 169-point drubbing of Woodville in 1970 is that club's GWM. South Adelaide's 130-point win (1965) is their GWM.

Woodville own 4 of the SANFL's lowest 25 scores post-1964.

Woodville finished above 8th only 4 times in their history.

WOODVILLE — WEST TORRENS

Only new and with nowhere near the endearing, yet hopeless, efforts of their progenitors to boast of, the Eagles appear to have taken off.

Percentage lost of all games played	33
Percentage of all finals lost	55
Percentage of Grand Finals lost	50
Worst flag drought	2yrs
Current flag drought	2yrs
Longest losing sequence	6
Lowest score	3.9 v North, 1995
Wooden spoons	0

REFERENCES

AFL Media Guide.

Agars, Merv, *Bloods Sweat and Tears,* The West Adelaide Football Club, 1987.

Bartlett, Kevin, *Kevin Bartlett's book of Football*, The Five Mile Press, 1995.

Casey, Kevin, *The Tigers' Tale,* Claremont Football Club, 1995.

Christian, Geoff, *The Footballers*, St George Books, 1985, revised edition, 1988.

Coward, Mike, *Men Of Norwood — The Red and Blue Blooded*, Norwood Football Club, 1992.

Dyer, Jack and Hansen, Brian, *Captain Blood's Wild Men of Football,* Vol 1, Brian Edward Hansen, 1993.

Dyer, Jack and Hansen, Brian, *Captain Blood's Wild Men of Football,* Vol 2, Brian Hansen Publications, 1994.

Handley, George, *The Great Grand Finals,* Walshe Publishing, 1989.

Hansen, Brian, *The Magpies — The Official Centenary History of the Collingwood Football Club,* Brian Hansen and Senis Carla Nominees Pty Ltd, 1992.

Hayman, Dion and Russo, Steve, *The Complete Book of SANFL Records*, Dion Hayman and Steve Russo, 1990.

Keenan, Peter, *Crackers, The Peter Keenan Story,* as told to Simon Townley, ABC Enterprises, 1990.

Lee, Jack, *Old Easts, 1948-1975,* East Fremantle Football Club, 1976.

Main, Jim and Holmesby, Russell, *The Encyclopedia of League Footballers,* Wilkinson Books, 1994.

Piesse, Ken, *The Complete Guide to Australian Football,* Ironbark, 1993, reprinted 1995.

Wood, John, *The Centenary History of The North Adelaide Football Club Inc,* North Adelaide Football Club, 1993.